"My wish is that you could hear Matt in person, delivering the message of this book. Written words do not give full expression to the breadth of his vision, the intensity of his passion or the depth of his devotion to bringing to the world the truest possible representation of Jesus Christ. There is enough here, however, to catch you on fire. In Change Together, Matt challenges us with a Biblical design of engaging the supernatural life of God in natural human experience. In everyday actions that, if not easy are nevertheless simple, the ordinary Christian becomes an extraordinary agent of change.

Is it possible for believers today to move beyond quoting John 3:16 and join God in his love for the world? Matt shows us that it is not only possible, but in clearly practical ways, it is doable. Do not read this book if you're a Christian who is content to settle into a comfortable, sterile life. If you are ready to get up and do something for heaven's sake, read it."

Chuck Smith, JR
Author, There Is A Season

"Matt Whitlock, a friend, a man of vision, passion for the Great Commission of Jesus, and a man of action. When he speaks or writes I listen!"

Dr. Loren Cunningham
Founder, Youth With A Mission (YWAM)

"Whenever people speak of missions or missionaries, the conversation usually ushers a sense of awe or even reverence. Certainly, it's important, but it's dangerous when we think that missions is something we do exclusively 'over there' and that the call of missionaries are only reserved for spiritual giants. I don't want to dismiss the importance of missions and missionaries. In fact, I want to emphatically affirm its importance. But, we desperately need a more robust and holistic missiology that includes our local contexts and also invites and challenge each follower to embody a 'missionary lifestyle.' This is why Change Together is such an important book.

Matt Whitlock has written an incredibly insightful, accessible, and practical book that will both challenge and encourage every follower of Christ. As we support and pray for the work of global missions, we need every believer to also commit themselves as a lifestyle missionary - wherever they may be planted."

Rev. Eugene Cho
Pastor and Founder, One Day's Wages
Author, Overrated: Are We More in Love With the Idea of
Changing the World Than Actually Changing the World?

"For far too long Christianity has been stuck in a weekend service. And "missions" is something that a few courageous—or crazy—people do in distant lands. In Change Together, Matt shows us how we were all meant to be on this journey together and that Jesus always intended that missions be a lifestyle, not a trip overseas! This book will push your boundaries in the best possible way."

Caesar Kalinowski
Author, Gospel Primer, Transformed and Bigger Gospel

"It is past time for Christians to stop talking about 'full time Christian ministry' as only applying to some, but not all, Christ-followers. To be a Christian is to be on mission, and few have articulated this truth better than Matt Whitlock has in this book. I pray it is widely read, and sparks the imagination of Christians everywhere to see their lives in the Kingdom terms described here."

John Stonestreet
President, Colson Center for Christian Worldview
Co-author, A Practical Guide to Culture

"My grandfather was a missionary for 40 years, serving in Angola, Africa. For many years, I served on the board of a mission organization, and I've traveled to over forty countries meeting people doing mission work. So, I've known a lot of missionaries. But if there's one missionary I could introduce you to who could show you, by example, how to live a missionary lifestyle, it would be Matt Whitlock. Next best thing to meeting him? You can read his book. It's well-written. It's down-to-earth. And it's what Christians around the world today need."

Brian D. McLaren
Author, The Great Spiritual Migration

"Change Together is a manifesto for followers of Jesus to take up the call to 21st century missions work—right where we have been placed."

Gabe Lyons
President, Q Ideas
Author, Good Faith & The Next Christians

"The life story of Matt Whitlock is uniquely powerful. He is a man who understands seasons and relevance and has a deep passion for enriching and equipping others for soul winning. His work and insight is truly amazing and inspirational. For me, this book defines the idea of God's blessing being dispersed locally and globally through His people in a 'lifestyle missionary' framework like that of Jesus. For those of you who have received a calling from God in evangelism leadership, you have the right book in your hands. It will inspire and move you through workable evangelism strategies and clear steps to achieving fruitfulness through biblical wisdom in winning souls. As you read, capture and contemplate its essence. Then, you will be determined to move into effective life practices."

Billy Sindoro
Lead Pastor, Christ Cathedral Church, Jakarta, Indonesia

"Always illuminating and instructive, Whitlock shows how a missionary life-style can become a whole life-story of radiance and significance. His skill at cross-cutting the personal with the biblical and the theological is a model for all writers."

Leonard Sweet
Best-selling author, Tablet to Table
Professor
George Fox University, Tabor College, Drew University
Founder of preachthestory.com

CHANGE TOGETHER
Seven Practices of a Lifestyle Missionary

By Matt Whitlock

ACKNOWLEDGMENTS

First and foremost, I would like to thank our heavenly Father. God as my Father has meant a great deal to me. Thank you to my mother who gave birth to me and has always had my back. A special thank you to my wife, Mina, and our children for being patient with me, and helping me form this message. We have traveled around the world together several times, inspiring the body of Christ with it.

I would like to thank Chuck Smith Jr, Loren and Darlene Cunningham, Brian D. Molitor, and Craig Whittaker for specifically having a dramatic impact at different stages in my adult life. I would not be where I am today without them, and I'll do my best to follow their example.

Lastly, to all my friends and coworkers around the world: I often have said that God can potentially speak at least seven billion different ways because He speaks through His creation and each person is uniquely created. As you read this book, I know you will hear a bit of your voice. Thanks to each and every one of you for sharing with me your story, idea, and inspiration. I was listening and touched deeply by it.

contents

Introduction

Five years ago I was called into a meeting. It wasn't a board meeting nor was it a casual coffee meeting. It was the kind of meeting where someone had a desire to confront me about something. Of course, it wasn't my favorite kind of meeting.

I sat down in the conference room. It was a long room to fit the extra long board room table. The lighting was dim and it carried the eerie feeling of a dramatic movie. Almost as soon as I sat down the young man who'd called the meeting, moved in close and began to berate me about my lack of holiness. I was so confused about what was even happening. I didn't know Adam. He was a part of the same missions' organization, but we didn't have a friendship. But I listened.

Adam placed his hands on the table and leaned forward. "Matt, I read through your blog, and all I found was secular music and movies with comments you had written about how you could hear Jesus in the music and movies." He leaned back and crossed his arms with his chest puffed out and a stern scowl. "We strive for holiness around here, and your lack of holiness is clearly illustrated in your posts."

I was shocked. Apparently, he had come across a blog that I had written a year previous to this meeting. In that blog post I had taken a controversial secular music video and pointed out that though not created for Christians, it had contained some biblical truth. I did this often in my blogs in order to help my non-Christian friends see truth about God even in popular culture. Adam was not particularly fond of the ideas mentioned in my blog and felt I had crossed an invisible heretic line in my theology.

I've always done my best to inspire the church to move outside of its walls and into the streets. Ten years ago I was speaking to a group of several hundred people who were training to be missionaries at youth with a mission (YWAM). My goal was to let them know that the pulpit was meant to be their lives and not a wooden object on a stage. I had found an old wooden pulpit in the back room earlier, so to further communicate this point, while I was in the middle of preaching, a friend of mine stepped onstage and handed me a revving chainsaw. To everyone's shock, I sawed the pulpit in half right on the stage. You can imagine how glorious it was with chips of wood and sawdust flying everywhere as I blasted through the pulpit with a massive chainsaw.

After I had finished, I picked up a piece of wood and then did an altar call for those who wanted to strive to make their lives their pulpits not a stage and microphone. Great demonstration, right? Well, the majority of the crowd enjoyed it, but not everyone appreciated my demonstration. Had I done a little research, I would have found that there was a Korean pastors' seminar in attendance in the front row that night. They graciously declined the altar call.

I had spent the better part of my twenties trying to help the church see a different side of "missions". Much of that time was an exploration of personal application as well as inspiring others. I wrote a book, blogs, made short videos, and used whatever medium possible to inspire the church to reach their neighbors.

As I sat across from Adam, I couldn't help but shake my head. At that time, I had just spent more than five years church-planting in California. The only Christian friends I had during that time were those with whom I was a part of their salvation experience. I was deep—deep in culture representing and

12

communicating Christ. My audience was completely different in California, and I was doing my best to help the church be "known for what they were for, not for what they were against."

But there I was getting berated because my efforts were not deemed "holy." While I envisioned myself jumping across the table and physically harming this young man, I retrained myself and listened. In that moment, I realized that even though everything I had done was meant to inspire people like him— young men and women who represent the church—I was not accomplishing my goal because he was so deeply offended by my past actions.

While a little controversy and drama is good and needed at times in order to see things in a contrasting light, I might have leaned too far with my blogs, creative sermons and innovative ministry endeavors. And that was when it hit me: in a twist of irony I had actually become "known more for what I was against then what I was for." I left that meeting realizing I needed to change my approach.

When I was eighteen years old, I embarked on a spiritual journey that would forever change my life, my worldview, and my relationship with Jesus Christ. I had joined Youth With A Mission and studied and learned what it meant to be a minister of the Word. Over the next twenty years, I have traveled around the globe ministering in over 50 nations, wrote books, blogs and created media all around the idea of inspiring people to join God's mission. Over the last 10 years God has been guiding my family and I into a greater understanding that His mission is active and within arms reach. My hope is by sharing some of that journey in the pages of this book it, would inspire you to the reality that God is calling you to join that mission too!

As you read this I'm about to turn forty years young and

I have a deep desire to truly inspire the church. My hope for this book is that it encourages you to see a broader picture of your faith. There will be times when you won't agree with me, but I'm okay with that if you're okay with that. It's in that tension that hopefully something beautiful will arise. Yet I call upon you, dear reader, to join me and thousands of others around the world who have made it our lifestyle to be missionaries. Each chapter will focus on specific practices to help start you on a journey of joining the mission of Jesus around you. One thing we can all agree on is that Jesus Christ is our axiom in this life. My hope is that you will see how He is calling you right now into that simple yet profound mission of sharing the good news.

Can you hear it?

one
A Lifestyle

I would never forget the day when I stood in front of the mirror holding my dad's electric razor. The beard-trimmer blade was extended and I felt ready. Something about the buzz of the razor when I flicked it on told me that this was a defining moment. I was thirteen years old, and crossing this threshold was already changing my self-perception. I was transitioning through a sort of straight-edge rite of passage.

As I look back at my early teens, I can see how I was beginning to form an identity, although at that time my friends and I were not thinking in terms of identity, nor was its formation on our to-do list. The one thing I knew for certain was that the world of skateboarding had me locked in its tractor beam. By the time I came around to it, skateboarding was dead (or it was passing through a liminal phase). The big ramps disappeared and mass media had turned its focus on other trends. Skateboarding returned to the streets where it began. It gathered more serious followers who never considered it a fad or even a sport. It was a way of life and I was a skater!

This radical commitment to a lifestyle was something I admired about skateboarders. Every day I skated as much as possible practicing my ollies, grinds, and flips, and I felt like I had found myself. I not only identified with skateboarding, but it had become a big part of my identity, which affected what I wore, the language I used, and the music that expressed my outlook and attitude that "Skateboarding is not a crime." Anyone could recognize the core skateboarders in the food court at the mall, even if we were not carrying our boards, which was rare. What gave us away was the massively oversized clothes that hung from our skinny teenage frames and hair that was long on top but shaved around the sides, not a tapered fade, but more like a Mohawk lying flat.

Today, lifestyle brands—that is, marketing accessories to a defined subculture—is a common theme. It seems that consumers want customization. Small is the new big. Orange is the new black. Hybrid is the new way of life. People do not think of themselves as taking up a hobby, indulging in a pastime, or flirting with art or music. Instead, people get serious about their pursuits. They are looking to integrate what matters most to them into a coherent and fulfilling lifestyle.

Ask any one of my Christian friends, "Are you religious?" He or she will most likely say something like, "No, I'm in a relationship with God." This is an important distinction. What's equally important is that we not think of ourselves as using our spare time for Christian activities, but as having adopted a lifestyle of faith. This does not mean that we accessorize to look like the brand; on the contrary, we choose the more serious path every day, an all-in devotion to following Jesus.

When I emphasize Christianity as a lifestyle, I am saying "no" to a status-quo life of mediocrity. When Jesus says, "Follow me," what I hear in His voice is not an invitation to attend a fun, hip event, but the challenge to devote my whole life to something that matters. Imagine what it would be like if we were to take the teachings of Jesus literally. I am quite sure we would be broke, as we would have gotten into the habit of giving away everything that came into our hands. Imagine our exhaustion from being compelled by compassion, which is part of God's Spirit, to always be responsive to human need. Our caloric intake would be low, not from pious fasting, but because our service to others would mean that we would frequently miss meals. However, it is likely that we would discover a new source of energy through God's Spirit empowering and sustaining us.

Many times, I have longed for the courage to be as unapologetic, politically incorrect, and intensely devout as Paul, James, Peter, and John were. Certainly, I'm closer than I used to be, but I still have a long way to go. In the meantime, the imperative of the Christian faith remains: Jesus Christ is the center of our life in God. The goal of discipleship is a lifestyle in which everything is oriented to Him, His word, and His will.

Devotion Looks Something like This

Among the plains tribes in the nineteenth century, the Cheyenne warriors were perhaps the most dangerous and most feared. These skilled fighters won not only the admiration of other tribe members but a place among the "Dog Soldiers," the name given to their warriors. Typically, training for the Dog Soldiers began when they were still children. When they came of age, they learned how to paint their bodies for battle, sing war cries, and whistle a unique sound. No doubt their enemies were terrified as the Dog Soldiers approached and their war cries rang out. Perhaps the most fascinating weapon in their arsenal was their sash and the sacred arrow.

Every Dog Soldier wore a sash around his waist or chest. Upon reaching the battlefield, they would drive the sacred arrow through an extended part of their sash and into the ground. This was not a verbal act, a vow, or promise of commitment, but a physical self-restraint sign to ensure they would fight to the death. Theirs was a "no retreat" strategy. Once they had engaged the enemy, there was no turning back. This personal act of total commitment differs from when commanders would land on enemy shores and order their ships to be burned. In those instances, the choice of no escape from battle had been made for the soldiers. Every Dog Soldier had to make the decision for himself.

What would motivate a warrior to make this kind of all-in commitment? Realistically, perhaps one in a thousand would do so for the glory or valor or even the prize of freedom. However, almost every man and woman would do it to protect what they loved: their way of life, their home, children, friends, or neighbors. The same is true of martyrs who, even today, are dying in many parts of the world. They hold on to their faith to the death for what they love and value. We cannot help but wonder how we would react if the knife were at our throats. Yet losing one's life to gain life was Jesus' requirement from those who wanted to follow Him.

The point is not that God wants everyone who believes in Him to be tortured or killed. His desire is not that we die but live. In fact, He desires that we live fully to the last breath. As the saying goes, "If nothing in our lives is big enough to be worth dying for, then neither is it worth living for."

"Follow Me... and No U-Turns"

Recently I was invited to a conference in Norway to address the graduating seniors in high school at the end of their last semester. It was just prior to "*russefering*," the equivalent of what goes on in the States during spring break. The *russ* celebration has been described as "part road trip, part rave, part high school graduation, and full lunacy." The partying goes on for about a month, during which the students wear wild overalls purchased from an online catalogue. People spend thousands of dollars fixing up and painting party buses that they ride from one city to another, celebrating the entire time.

The conference was designed as an alcohol and drug-free event for young people who wanted to have fun and be equipped to use their vacation time to introduce their friends to Jesus. I was asked to deliver a message to these teenagers to prepare them for the work they were about to undertake. I found myself standing before a crowd of more than seven hundred teenagers who were about to fix their sashes to the ground in the heart of the craziness and fight for the souls of their friends.

We ended the conference with an old-school altar call, inviting everyone who wanted to receive prayer for courage, wisdom, and effectiveness to stand up. After praying God's grace over them, we sang the perfect song:

> If I grow weary I still will follow.
> If I grow weary, I still will follow.
> If I grow weary, I still will follow;

No turning back, no turning back.
I have decided to follow Jesus.
I have decided to follow Jesus.
I have decided to follow Jesus;
No turning back, no turning back.

Here is the heart of following Jesus with the lifestyle to which we are called. We start with faith that never promised to be easy, take the uncertain paths that reveal God's will, and face the harrowing challenges that will define us. We have chosen a lifestyle through which the infinite God reveals His love for His finite creation. We have decided not to conform to the values of our transitory culture but to live the remainder of our lives in the eternal now—the intersection between calendar time and God's time as it presses into this present moment. With the eternal now perspective and experience, we confidently continue to go forward because we are not looking "at the things which are seen, but at the things which are not seen; for the things which are seen are temporal, but the things which are not seen are eternal" (2 Corinthians 4:18).

This is the lifestyle Jesus has in mind for us and to which we have been called.

two
A Missionary

One afternoon, when I was fourteen years old, I was riding bikes with my friends up and down my street. The day was hot and sweat trickled on my brow. I had almost reached the end of the street when I heard my mother calling my name.

I sighed and pedaled toward the house. "What, Mom?" I yelled. I was having fun and didn't want to leave my friends.

"We want you to come inside," she answered.

"Fine," I mumbled under my breath, then reluctantly said good-bye to my friends. As I headed for the front door, I could see from the look on her face that Mom was upset and had been crying. Immediately I assumed it was about me and the news was not good.

I walked slowly into the living room as Mom trailed behind me. Dad was sitting on the couch, waiting. Having an overactive imagination, I thought the worst. For some reason, I thought they were going to announce that I had contracted AIDS and only had a short time to live. Looking back, I don't know why I thought that or why that popped into my head at the time, but no matter our age, fear can take on many forms.

I sat down on the sofa across from my parents and before either of them could speak, I said, "It's okay. I already know what you're going to tell me."

My mother's eyes widened in shock. "Wait... how do you already know, Matt?"

"I figured it out by the look on your face," I told her. Just then, fear wrapped itself around me and a chill crawled up my spine. I was so afraid. "Please, just tell me how much time do I have left?"

Mom furrowed her brow in confusion. "What are you talking about?"

"It's okay. I learned all about this in school. I get it, I have AIDS, so just tell me how long I have before I die."

My parents erupted in laughter. Dad said, "No, Matthew, you do not have AIDS and you're not going to die. That's not what we need to tell you." Then, they revealed why they had wanted to talk to me.

My parents knew a young woman who had found herself in an impossible situation. Sadly, she'd been a victim of date rape, an all too common crime. Several weeks after that trauma, the young woman learned that she was pregnant. Given her circumstances, she saw no option other than abortion. On the day of the scheduled procedure, she was walking down a hall to the pre-op room and noticed a poster on the wall that illustrated the fetal development of an infant. In that moment, she recognized that what was growing within her was a baby, and she sensed a presence behind her—the presence of something great. Not having a relationship with God other than at Christmas or Easter, she was not sure what it was that she'd felt, but she quietly asked, "God, is that you?"

A nurse who was standing in front of the room called her name, so the young woman headed toward the room. The nurse greeted her and told her to undress and that she would be back in a moment. The young woman stood in the room alone, feeling confused. Quickly she put on the hospital gown, her body shaking from the cold and maybe something else, and she sat on the examination table and reflected on the strong sensation that had come over her only a few minutes earlier. Again, she breathed a silent prayer, "Lord, if that was you and I'm supposed to keep this child, I need your help right now!"

Just then, a surge of courage coursed throughout her body and she stood up, her feet and legs much steadier. Without hesitation, she took off the hospital gown and changed back into her own clothing. When the nurse returned she looked confused and asked what was going on. "I can't do this!" the woman adamantly replied, and she walked out.

That young woman was my mom. I was the child who narrowly missed being aborted.

After they divulged their secret, I was at a loss as to how I should respond, so I asked, "Can I go back outside now?" I climbed back onto my bike and rejoined my friends.

"What was that about?" my friend Johnny asked.

Still stunned, I answered, "Oh, they just wanted to tell me that my dad is not my real father."

Johnny gave me a confused look and asked, "Well, can you hang outside for a while longer?"

"Sure," I answered, and off we rode on our bikes.

Later that evening, I mulled over the revelation I had

received earlier. A thousand questions flooded my mind. *What does this mean? What has changed now that I know this information? Am I a different person now? What's my real biological background? Who am I?* Only later did I learn that philosophers have tried to answer these fundamental type of questions for centuries and most people ask these types of questions at some point in their lives. At that time, however, I remembered feeling curious as to how I should feel about learning that what I had considered a stable reality was not really true. Oddly, rather than being shaken by this sudden discovery, I felt a deep sense of peace. Wherever I had come from, God had my future in hand, otherwise, He would not have called me to Himself and given me a new life in Jesus Christ.

What I would later begin to realize is that my life was spared because Jesus was on mission and my mother was the object of his affection despite her current state of unbelief. While we might feel as though we are bringing Jesus into dark places, in actuality, He is already there calling for us to join Him on His mission. That understanding has been liberating as I now know it is His mission, not mine, and I'm following Him, not vice-versa.

A Heart for the Field

When it was time for me to choose a career path, it made perfect sense to become a missionary. Maybe it was me deep desire to be in extreme situations. Or the fact that I carried a deep conviction that my life was not my own. I had rehearsed the story of how I was conceived in my head a thousand times. I concluded the best way to show my gratitude was to give my life to the service of others. The difficult situations that discouraged others from traversing continents to interact with and learn from cultures very different from my own excited me. Sleeping on floors, unsanitary conditions, living on a diet of foreign food, sweating through long humid days, and doing whatever it took to extend the message of Jesus Christ to the farthest reaches of the earth were perks rather than deterrents. After all it was this Jesus who saved my life, literally. The future I envisioned for myself was radical, inconvenient, exhausting, and peppered with unforeseen challenges. I was not noble, foolhardy, or looking for pain, but I knew my calling. My heart had been prepared by God to find joy in a simple rugged existence. From my earliest experiences, the feeling that the work in the field evoked for me was, "I was made for this!" I even loved the all-or-nothing commitment that missionaries made when they allowed what was familiar to them to become strange so all that was strange could become familiar.

Immediately after finishing high school I had started to travel extensively in Central and South America and throughout the Asian and the African continents. In each place I was either introducing people to Jesus or teaching believers how to interpret the Scriptures, assisting local churches and humanitarian organizations, or training pastors to become church planters. After traveling the world working as a wild eyed young missionary in my mid-twenties, a realization began to dawn on me.

Although the label "missions" is usually the label for the work I was doing in foreign countries, was I doing anything I should not have been doing in my own country? There has always been a certain mystique about the word "missionary," but it simply refers to someone who is doing somewhere else what the rest of us should be doing at home. Only here, we are ordinary Christians doing what God has called us to do rather than calling ourselves "missionaries." I started wondering whether we should be using the term missionaries for everyone! As I saw could there be missionaries to academics at universities, or to the executives or managers in the corporate world, or to civil servants in the various levels of government. Why not?

A Real-Life Example

I first met Brian Molitor in my early twenties when he was guest lecturing at a Christian businessmen gathering in Hawaii, and I got to know him when we went fishing together. Brian is the CEO of Molitor International a Michigan based consulting firm that provides training for corporations and businesses. Rather than coming off as a hardheaded business type, he is more like an open-hearted father. One organization he founded is called the Malachi Global Foundation. The name is from a passage in which God promised to send Israel a prophet who would "restore the hearts of the fathers to their children and the hearts of the children to their fathers" (Malachi 4:6). Brian is passionate about his vision of healing fractured relationships between fathers and their sons or daughters. He has a way of making everyone he meets feel accepted, important, and valued. Soon after our first meeting, I discovered that he even believed in me in spite of myself.

Brian does not leave his spiritual values at the gate when he enters the corporate world. He is convinced that a Christian's lifestyle, especially one's interactions with people who cross his or her path, is the best way to introduce the kingdom of God in places where it is most needed. This particular facet of his lived-out faith interested me the most. Trusting myself to his gracious nature, I asked Brian, "Is there any way that I could learn leadership skills from you?" I was interested in applying his leadership skills to my own lectures on faith and real life practice of that faith. I saw a real felt need for people in different cultures to learn how to lead according to the model of Jesus.

Knowing that I was already teaching in several biblical courses, Brian handed me three leadership-training manuals and said, "Read these and let me know if you can teach this material."

I answered, "I can teach anything I believe in."

What followed was a crash course in corporate development. At his invitation, I joined him and hung out with the big boys at a training event in Midland, Michigan, to test my aptitude to learn the ropes.

My total wardrobe of dress clothes included one button-down shirt, one pair of khakis, and one pair of long socks. That was my uniform the day I entered corporate America. For three days, I sat in a room with business professionals while lecturers downloaded the organizational techniques Brian's company had developed over the course of thirty years. Everything that was shared on best leadership practices clicked for me. Perhaps it made sense because I had been traveling the world and had made every mistake imaginable while leading in a variety of different leadership structures. Seeing the right way to get things done effectively fit like keys in the locks I had picking.

After the conference, I made my way to Brian's office—stomach churning, palms sweating—and knocked on the door. After sitting down, I looked at him and said, "Brian, I have one question: Is there room for me in this organization?" He just looked at me with a question mark on his face, so I said, "I'm not sure what to say, but I need to know if there's room for me here." Then he smiled. After that day, I began working for Molitor International as an organizational development consultant, and I spent many productive and happy years working there.

Before I began, I had to get a couple of suits, the first

installment in creating an image of someone who would teach corporate executives. The average age of a consultant was fifty-five and I was a mature twenty-three year old. Secondly, Brian gave me further instructions: "Put on some weight. Don't tell anyone how old you are. Teach the material. Include illustrations or examples that indicate how much of the world you've traveled. Do these things and you'll be okay."

One day Brian and I went to a meeting with the CEO of a credit union bank and his executive team. Even though I was out of my league, I had confidence in Brian and the leadership training material I had taught. Before long Brian had me training leaders and managers in two companies. Through my interaction with these people, I realized that this was where the lost men and women in the countries of the world were hiding. We had not been able to coax them into our churches, concerts, or community events. The everyday workplace loomed before me as a large mission field into which millions of Christians enter.

However, therein lies a problem. These same believers who enter the domestic mission field every day did not consider themselves as missionaries. They assumed they were average Christians whose "secular" work was of no use to God or to the church. It only served to put food on the table. As far as mission work was concerned, they would put a few dollars in the offering basket or send a donation to support people like me once in a while. Weren't we, the believers, those who were "called" to carry God's good news to the lost masses in all lands?

A Church Planted in the Field

The church is God's gift to broken people. The church is a sanctuary from the chaos, conflict, and heartache of the world.

We bring our questions, doubts, and despair to the church and meet Jesus Christ. We bring our lonely souls to the church and receive the embrace of others. We bring our sicknesses to the church and receive healing. We bring our poverty to the church and are given food and clothing.

The church is a fountain of help for broken people. But now we must pay careful attention to what this means. The stories of healing that we read in the gospels reveal a healer who restored people not only to wholeness but also to productivity. The completeness that Christians obtain in Jesus can be instant. Nothing needs to be added to our faith as we receive His life, death, and resurrection. Our spiritual growth, however, is a long process. We should not think even for a moment that God must complete His work in us before He is willing to use us. Far from it. This means that while we are receiving so many spiritual benefits from the church, it does not exist to be a fortress against the world in which we spend our lives seeking advances week after week. To come at it from another angle, the mission of a healthy church is to be a service to those within it and those outside it.

Every Christian is a missionary. Why would I say this? Because every Christian is a follower of Jesus Christ. Christ's mission was to come into the world and reveal the heavenly Father to His estranged sons and daughters and reconcile them to Himself (2 Corinthians 5:19). I hope you can discern the difference between what I am saying and what we have heard from preachers and evangelists. I am not saying that we have this overwhelming responsibility of winning the world to Jesus Christ. I am saying that Jesus is in the world and He is inviting us to join Him on His mission. The work is His and He will see that it gets done. The Spirit of God works in human hearts to "convict the world concerning sin and righteousness and judgment" (John

16:8).

A professor of missiology in a US seminary had spent a couple of weeks at a conference in Nigeria where he was one of the speakers. During a dinner celebration at the last night of the conference, he asked one of his hosts, "Is there anything you want me to tell the young missionaries I am training when I return home?" His host replied, "Yes. Please tell them that they are not bringing God to Nigeria, but that God is bringing them to Nigeria." Is God at home in Nigeria? Of course.

We all need to see ourselves as missionaries since we are the people who enter these everyday environments who know Jesus. We are the light of the world, which we show in our daily routine. So, whether I am a mom with two small children at the park, a student pursuing a degree, a schoolteacher, a skateboarder, an Internet gaming geek, I will always come into contact with people who are objects of Jesus' mission regardless of what I do and wherever I go. Can you see that He has His reasons for placing you right there among them?

Jesus' mission is one of restoration. This is an especially important concept for me since it is a reminder that there is something good and right about each person and that a smoldering ember can be made to burn again. Irenaeus, a theologian of the second and third centuries, commented on humankind being made in the "image and likeness" of God and taught that the image of God cannot be erased. It defines the human person, but the likeness of God in a person was lost in the fall. What is restored when we came to Christ is God's likeness. Whether or not this is so, Irenaeus has a point: all humans bear God's image; salvation is the restoration to our original design and intention. We need to beware of terminology that implies that non-Christians are a total loss.

Before the earth was created, God chose us to become the products of His craftsmanship. Sin, however, was the monkey wrench that sabotaged God's handiwork. You have probably heard that sin means "to miss the mark." The mark was God's destiny for each of us. Missing the mark, we lost not only our destiny but our true identity as well. Jesus Christ came to restore us to God and to our true selves. When we are expressions of God's creativity inspiring and empowering our creativity, we become His handiwork. A transformed life is something beautiful and serves to attract others to Jesus. This is where missions combine with lifestyle so that our vocation as a witness becomes more important than our career. There will always be some of us called to foreign missions as career missionaries. However, all of us are called to be missionaries in our different everyday careers.

Stories with Intent is an exhaustive commentary on the parables of Jesus. Klyne Snodgrass, a theologian and professor, concludes his thoughts on the parable of the talents (Matthew 25:14–20; Luke 19:11–27) by stating in his book, "The parable urges readiness, preparedness, in view of the coming of the kingdom." He goes on to state, "Readiness is an attitude, a commitment, and a lifestyle." Exactly! "Missionary" is a divisive term; people tend to either love missionaries or hate them. Missionaries have been agents of change in the world. Sometimes they have been agitators and other times catalysts. Missionaries were the only ones who carried their coffins into remote regions, uncertain of whether they would ever return to their native country. Missionaries were those who risked everything. Missionaries made change happen.

My deepened perspective sees that Jesus is on a mission all around us and He has invited us to join Him. Consider this: No one handed my mom a religious tract, nor was she listening to a radio or TV preacher. The nurse didn't share the gospel with her either. But a moment came when my mother's heart opened and was invaded by the mission of Jesus, which in turn saved my life. This is why I cannot believe we have joined a happy-clappy self-help club; we have joined a mission. A mission this intense and serious has little to do with creating a "cool" church, but everything to do with the nature of our God. We do not have to search for the perfect location; we need only be concerned with the orientation of our hearts.

When my friends and I got together to talk about the new thing God is doing in our world today, we coined the term "Lifestyle Missionary." You might be wondering what a Lifestyle Missionary believes and how do they live. To help break this term down a bit, we created this manifesto.

Lifestyle Missionary Manifesto

We are determined to live out the goodness of God on Earth.

Who are we? We are game-changers, playmakers, box-breakers, and risk-takers. We are a global family of visionary practitioners, poets, preachers, and pioneers. We are sons and daughters. We are blessed to be a blessing, loved to be lovers, freed to be liberators, and called to rise above the status quo.

This is what we believe: Every follower of Jesus, by default, is part of God's trajectory of restoration. This mission requires active participation as we become the incarnation of love in a broken world. Being fully equipped by the Holy Spirit, we are united with one purpose expressed in infinitely diverse vocations. We are convinced that God's mission is simple, collaborative, and within arm's reach.

This is how we choose to live: We embrace inconvenience, listen deeply, honor all, and live generously. We focus our energy locally yet still engage globally. We open our hearts, homes, and lives to all people in courageous acts of hospitality. When we gather we eat well, we pray expectantly, and we learn Scripture. We will leave our communities better than when we found them. We will promote peace, pursue unity, and protect the vulnerable. Last but not least, we seek God's kingdom before our own.

We hereby declare a new era in which these are our defining characteristics. An era in which we will shape culture together as an unstoppable surge of ordinary people. Through faithful presence and collaborative obedience, we will see God's kingdom come here and now.

We are a global family of Lifestyle Missionaries.

In heaven, it will be obvious that God's work was not carried forward by a handful of superstars for each generation, but by the culmination of all the prayers and efforts of every ordinary believer doing the simple things that gave birth to the extraordinary results. As my friend Tommy says, "Many hands make light work!"

three
Practice #1: Pray Expectantly

"If prayer has any reality at all, it is founded upon a sense of God, and as it develops into something more than an occasional spasmodic cry under the pressure of need or anguish, our sense of God becomes a dominant factor in our lives."
– Emily Herman, Creative Prayer

Our experience is of this present moment. Past moments have fallen into history, and future moments are hidden in mystery. Our encounter with "reality" is in this moment alone. Any residue of the past that lingers in our minds is memory, which to some degree always distorts reality. The future is nothing more than a cluster of possibilities. Any plans you may have for tomorrow are probabilities, because "you do not know what your life will be like tomorrow. You are just a vapor that appears for a little while and then vanishes away" (James 4:14). My encounter with reality is "right now" as I type these words, and for you it is "right now" as you read them. With the help of imagination, you can continue to relive regrets or resentments from the past or project anxieties into the future. Otherwise, you will never be closer to reality than you are now as you inhale your next breath.

The first message that Jesus delivered was, "The time is fulfilled, and the kingdom of God is at hand" (Mark 1:15). He did not say, "The time is coming," but that it was fulfilled. It had arrived. Nor did He say, "The kingdom of God is on its way," but "at hand." Toward the end of Mark's gospel, when Jesus told His disciples, "behold, the one who betrays Me is at hand," Judas had already entered Gethsemane. "Immediately while Jesus was still speaking, Judas, one of the twelve, came up accompanied by a crowd with swords and clubs…" (Mark 14:4-43). In a similar way, while Jesus was still announcing that the kingdom of God was at hand, it arrived with His words. Through Jesus Christ, the dimension of God was breaking into "this present evil age."

In His parables, Jesus explained the "mystery of the kingdom," how it could be present in the world now yet hidden from human eyes like a seed buried in the ground or yeast "hidden" in a lump of bread dough. Invisible but present, the kingdom of God was mysteriously growing and exercising a powerful and recognizable influence on those who met Jesus (cf. Matthew 13:31-33). When Jesus exorcised demons, it was evident that the kingdom of God was present (Luke 11:20) and for that reason He could say, "The kingdom of God is not coming with signs to be observed; nor will they say, 'Look, here it is!' or 'There it is!' For behold, the kingdom of God is in your midst" (Luke 17:20-21).

The conquest of sin and death is not yet complete, nor has the earthly reign of God come in all of its fullness. Nevertheless, the spiritual presence of God's realm is reaching humans as they hear and surrender to the message of Jesus. So Paul could say that God has "rescued us from the domain of darkness, and transferred us to the kingdom of His beloved Son" (Colossians 1:13). So much of what we hope to receive from God someday is not stowed away in an indefinite future. "Behold, NOW is the acceptable time; behold, NOW is the day of salvation" (2 Corinthians 6:2). We hope that someday we will have a stronger resistance to sin, a greater closeness to Jesus, a stronger evidence of God's work in our church, and a greater influence for God in our world. That is why we need to know what time it is, "…that it is already the hour for you to awaken from sleep for NOW salvation is nearer to us than when we believed" (Romans 13:11).

Freedom from the stranglehold of guilt and shame is ours NOW. God's love is ours NOW, and nothing can separate us from it. The life and power of God's Spirit are with us NOW. The reality of everything we desire to have in God for faith, healthy relationships, a God-filled lifestyle is ours NOW. Slowly take a deep breath, and before you exhale say, "now" and see if you can sense God's kingdom all around you. Welcome to the eternal now! The kingdom of God is hidden in every moment of our lives and we can pray expectantly from this place.

Time and Eternity

In the New Testament, two words are used to represent time. We are familiar with the Greek word "*chronos*" because it occurs in English words such as "chronic" (long lasting or recurring), "chronology," or "chronicle." *Chronos* is a linear time and moves sequentially from one event to another. We travel a horizontal timeline from birth to death, checking our calendars

37

to remind ourselves of where we are at chronos time.

The second Greek word for time is "*kairos*." However, it is used for a specific and special moment, an appointed time, an opportune time. *Kairos* is God's time, the powerful moments when He enters our lives and leaves us breathless, like Jacob after his dream of the ladder to heaven when he said, "Surely the LORD is in this place, and I did not know it" (Genesis 28:16). The unique moment of *kairos* is like a vertical line that intersects chronos time, and at that intersection, God draws near to us, and heaven touches Earth and grace meets faith. *Kairos* is the intersection of time and eternity. *Kairos* is always happening, but we are asleep to this reality.

We look down at our watches or scroll through our smartphones, and rush past *kairos* intersections without ever knowing that they exist. But these priceless moments of God's nearness are precisely our destination. If we are doing everything in Him, through Him, for Him, and by His strength, what better way is there to live than to be continuously mindful of His presence?

We go through an entire week and choose to wake up only for specific religious occasions—Sunday morning church, mid-week Bible study, prayer over our meals, or when we share our faith with someone who does not know God. Frequently, when we do wake up, we are amazed. We tell our friends of the wonderful way that God met us at church, and how everyone felt His presence and about the inspiration that now burns in our hearts.

There are other times, however, when we pray for God's blessings on our church service and sing songs to invite Him to come and meet with us, but it seems that nothing extraordinary happens. With perhaps a tinge of envy, we hear about the wonderful things that are happening in another church and we ask God why the life has leaked out of our own. I have heard Christian friends say, "God's Spirit is really moving at a church across town, but there's not a hint of His presence in ours."

We have to realize that God does not see what we see, that His thoughts are not our thoughts, and His ways are not our ways. God does not begin His day going over His to-do list or looking at the appointments on His day calendar. He does not schedule appearances in certain churches and turn down invitations to visit others. Whether we experience God in our church—or anywhere else—is not determined by a heavenly receptionist who books His appointments, but it is all about people who choose to wake up to the fact that He is already present with us. God draws near to the people who in faith are drawing near to Him. Expectation and wakefulness have more to do with our experience of God than the building where we meet, the preacher who speaks, or the band that leads worship. Religious occasions are not the only times in which God desires us to be alert to Him.

Reverence for Mystery

We live in an age of explanations—scientific explanations, rational explanations, medical explanations, sociological explanations, and biblical explanations. If there has been anything left unexplained, you can be certain that someone somewhere is searching for that explanation. The New Testament, however, makes no attempt to clarify everything. Have you ever noticed that Jesus rarely gave straight answers to direct questions? Perhaps He wanted people to know that they were asking the wrong questions. It is also possible that being with and pondering the right question was more important than having the "correct" answer. Jesus left room for mystery.

Jesus did not try to solve the "mystery of the kingdom of heaven" for everyone (Matthew 13:11-15). Paul described himself as a servant of Jesus Christ, but he also called himself and others "stewards of the mysteries of God" (1 Corinthians 4:1). What this probably meant was that the gospel Paul proclaimed was the based on "the revelation of the mystery which has been kept secret for long ages past" regarding the door that God had opened to the Gentiles to know Him through Jesus (Romans 16:25-26; Ephesians 3:1-7; Colossians 1:25-27). Nevertheless, Paul did not know "all mysteries" (1 Corinthians 13:2), nor did he try to figure out what every mystery meant. In fact, he said that some could not be spoken about. (1 Corinthians 15:51-57; 2 Corinthians 12:2-3).

We have Lost That Respect for Mystery

By and large, Evangelical Christians have a solid understanding of the theological truth that God is Person. This is apparent in the frequency with which we use the phrase, "Personal relationship with Jesus Christ," or our having a "relationship with God." This understanding allows us to worship God with songs that express our intimacy with Him. But in other parts of the world where Christianity has been opposed and believers have been persecuted and oppressed, we often see what it means to have a solid understanding of the theological truth that God is Mystery. What is striking about the worship of these believers is their deep respect for God, which is evident in their worship. It is a reverence that is lacking in much of our worship. Somehow we need to learn to pray and worship in the tension of God's nearness and in distance. His imminence and transcendence show us that

He is both Person and Mystery. We can retain reverence that rises from mystery if we remember that what we know about God is infinitely less than what there is to know. Simply reflecting on God's holiness is enough to make us tremble.

We have Lost That Mystery

It may be that recovering a sense of the mystery that surrounds our heavenly father will lead us back to a childlike faith, full of awe and wonder. We might discover that just as God is in every moment, His glory shines through every flower, tree, insect, and clump of dirt. Yes, the amazing sunset, the wind bending a palm tree, or the loud thunderclap will thrill us with the glory and power of our God. Maybe by seeing mystery in everything, we will learn a deeper spiritual sensitivity that recognizes God's touch in the small, ordinary, and simple things of our world.

We need to wake up.

Receptive and Responsive

I have been sketching the vision of a Lifestyle Missionary. Our time together in church is greatly enhanced because we bring our deepened sense of God's nearness with us. Then what we experience in word and worship in community will prepare us to live the word and worship all the other days of the week. The goal is to develop a stronger discipline of looking and listening. In the past, God's will for many of us has been a source of stress or anxiety. Could it be that we fear it or live in uncertainty as to what it is He wants us to do with our lives? By surrendering ourselves to Him in each moment, we will discover how He is directing us each day. It may be that God's will is not the big thing of our lifetime but many small things of each day.

We cannot pretend that a moment-to-moment surrender to the will of God is easy, because we sometimes walk with our heads down, wanting to be diverted by our "busy schedule." At times, God's mission comes to us when we find it tremendously inconvenient. So, occasionally, we have decided not to participate with God even when we can see clearly what He was doing.

A couple of years ago, I accepted an invitation to teach in my friend's church in South Korea. After one of my sessions, a church member said to me, "Matt, the stories you told about being a lifestyle missionary are really good, but do you have any stories where it didn't work out so well?" As a matter of fact, earlier that week I had experienced what I considered an epic fail.

My schedule in South Korea was crowded with meetings and speaking engagements, so I was super busy with hardly any time to myself. Whenever I had a few free minutes, I would try to squeeze in a jog or workout. One morning while I was running, I noticed an elderly woman in her late seventies struggling to carry a chair as she walked down the side of the road.

As I ran by, it was obvious to me that the right thing to do would have been to offer to help her. But I knew what would happen if I helped her, as the scenario through my head. First, I would have to carry the chair all the way to her destination. Then, she would graciously invite me to stay and courtesy would require that I would. Next, she would feed me and bring her family over to meet me. If they were Christians, we would talk about our faith. If they were not believers, then I would have an opportunity to share with them, and if they were receptive, it was possible that we would pray and ask Jesus to invade their lives, all of which would take a long time.

A glorious opportunity, right? Well, I just kept running

because I did not want to sacrifice the little bit of time I had to myself. Was God disappointed with me? I do not think so, but I'm not sure. And therein lies the problem. An opportunity was dropped in my path, and I dropped the ball. Our praying expectantly can rub our precious schedule. But in getting to know God more, we know that He never wastes anything. In this case, He gave me the opportunity to take a good long look at my heart.

But here's the hope. In John's gospel, Jesus came to the pools of Bethsaida inside the northeast walls of Jerusalem. Because people with various illnesses had been healed by entering the water there, "a multitude of those who were sick, blind, lame, and withered" were drawn there, hoping to have their turn. What happened then has always perplexed me. All these people surrounding the pool, looking for a miracle, yet Jesus spoke to only one man, healed him, and then Jesus went on His way. I imagine a disciple saying, "Uh, excuse me, Lord, but you didn't finish the work back there. All those other people would be grateful if you would touch them too." But Jesus had His own thoughts about what was the "one necessary thing" to do at Bethesda. In fact, His thoughts were to only do what He saw the Father doing (John 5:19).

In Acts chapter 3, Peter and John climbed the steps and approached the Beautiful Gate to enter the temple courts (Acts chapter 3). This occurred at the opposite end of the eastern wall in Jerusalem. A crippled man had spent many years outside the wall, begging the people who were going in to pray and worship. In a tremendously dramatic encounter, Peter healed the man, then Peter, John, and the healed man went into the temple. The man was "walking and leaping and praising God." What interests me about this scene is that those were the same steps Jesus would have had to climb every time He entered the temple, which would imply that He had passed by this man many times. If it was God's will to heal this man, why didn't Jesus perform the miracle? We can be sure that all three of them—Jesus, Peter, and John—were all listening to the Spirit of God as they headed into the temple. All three of them were devoted to doing the Father's will. But for reasons we don't know about, God had appointed the *kairos* moment of healing for this longtime crippled man to come at the perfect time in all their lives.

Jesus was a Listener

Jesus walked in the light and so He knew what to do with His twelve hours of daylight (John 11:9). Knowing that His hour to come forward, to reveal Himself, and to be "lifted up from the earth," was imminent, He neither rushed it nor dodged it (cf. John 7:6-8; 12:27-28). Always conscious of His Father's will, Jesus did only what He saw the Father doing: never too much or too little.

Jesus showed us how to walk out the Father's will. We are to be looking and listening, receptive and responsive, hearing and obeying. It is not only possible for us to have a keener awareness of God in the present moment, but it is imperative that we train our senses for this particular purpose. The mission, after all, is God's, not ours. We have been invited into partnership with Him. Small acts done by millions of Christians would totally change the world. We just need to be open to Him and join Him. The rest will unfold.

four
Practice #2: Live Scripture

Not long ago I was in Scandinavia on a speaking tour. One afternoon, I didn't have any appointments scheduled, so I decided to go to the cinema. (I will not mention the movie to spare you wasting spiritual energy judging me!) As is my habit, I like to get to movies on time. In fact, my ideal scenario is to arrive in the theater and be seated five minutes before the movie begins. I love watching the trailers.

That particular afternoon, I got to the theater much earlier than I expected, which meant I had to sit through a lot of advertisements in a language I did not speak. Because I had nothing else to do, I watched. One advertisement showed a Scandinavian hipster (you are familiar with this type of person; hipsters are an international phenomenon). He was wearing a knitted hat, skinny jeans, Converse tennis shoes and, of course, he had a beard. The commercial was extremely fast-paced, so much so that you were not able to follow it unless you recognized the icons that are familiar sights in every big city.

The commercial's storyline went like this: The hipster was a famous photographer in demand. He raced around the world shooting photos for high-end clients and good-looking men and women. After a whirlwind day with fabulous people, he returned to his penthouse apartment and went to the refrigerator, which was empty except for something in a crumpled wrapper. At this point, the soundtrack changed to the nostalgic sound of stringed instruments. He slowly pulled the wrapper out of the refrigerator, and as the camera moved in for a close-up, its mystery was revealed. The priceless treasure he held was "Norwegian Chocolate." As his teeth sunk into the chocolate, he was instantly transported back in time to a small fishing town in Norway. There, his father, dressed in jeans (that were not skinny jeans) and sporting a much longer beard than his son, stood waiting for him. Together they go fishing. Afterward they return home, where his mother had prepared a hearty meal. When he took a bite of the food, *poof* and he was back in his hotel suite. This wonderful moment of reverie was brought about by the workings of chocolate.

I understood the message perfectly because the story was told in pictures. No words were used other than the brand name on the wrapper. I found myself captivated by it. I wanted to go out and purchase that chocolate. Could it do all the wonderful things for me that it did for the actor? Could it ease my travel fatigue and make me feel like I was at home?

This is the genius of marketing. Advertisers convince us that the story they are telling is better than the one we are living. We see the ad and immediately we are tempted to buy the product. Why? Simply because we have been made in the image of a God who is writing us into the greatest story ever told. In our body and soul, we seek a wonderful adventure of risk and romance that brings us to the "happily ever after." Sadly, most of the time we are unaware of God's grand story and we have been written into its plot. Marketers, however, have learned to tap our core emotions and deepest longings. We are enchanted by their artificial stories because our souls are too sick to discover the real Divine Story.

We have contracted an illness that my friend, Len Sweet, refers to as "Verse-itis." Verse-itis is a disease of stunted spiritual growth that believers contract when they hold within them the greatest story "never" told. We work hard at getting the Bible into our heads without it penetrating our hearts. We memorize and recite our favorite verses—usually those that support arguments for our cherished beliefs—with the result that unreached people hear from us a small portion of the Bible, yet strive to see the whole of it in our lives. Unbelievers know us more for what we are against than what we are for. That is because we were led to believe that "personal evangelism" consists of spitting verses at people rather than learning and living the larger story, drawn from every chapter of every book. Too few Christians live the Scriptures in such a way that people become captivated by the story that unfolds before them. Because they do not see in Christians a spirit-inspired creativity, joyful exploration of truth, and enthusiastic determination, the Scripture parts they hear sound unconvincing and boring. They would rather live in the fantasy of the advertisers' story or write their own then join us in the live experience of God's story.

The Tragic Misrepresentation of God's Story

How did the church get to this place? First off, I think it

is important to realize a few things about the Bible.

Scripture is not a textbook or an encyclopedia, but a collection of stories.

Scripture is not written *to* you but *for* you.

Scripture reveals God's desire to recover, redeem, reconcile, and restore all things.

Scripture does not give us a religious code to follow, but a lifestyle to embrace and own.

Scripture is not a Textbook or an Encyclopedia but a Collection of Stories

One of the most common questions that pastors and Bible teachers are asked is, "What does the Bible say about _____?" (fill in the blank). What they expect to hear is one relevant verse or a string of verses with the precise answer. *Nave's Topical Bible* is a classic example of treating the Scriptures as if they only provided information or precise definitions regarding many different subjects and concepts. The Bible, however, is not one book, but a collection of many books, and not one of them was meant to be a dictionary. In fact, a large portion of the Bible consists of books that tell stories (Genesis through Esther—as much as eighty percent of the Old Testament—and Matthew through Acts in the New Testament). These stories involve ordinary people trying to work out what it means to be in a covenant relationship with an extraordinary God. The Bible contains other types of literature that includes the following:

Wisdom literature: for example, Proverbs and Ecclesiastes.

Prophetic literature: from the major and minor prophets of the Old Testament. A special class of prophetic literature has been labeled "apocalyptic," which is found in the Old Testament

Book of Daniel and the New Testament Book of Revelation. Some of the prophetic books contain predictions regarding future events, but not so much as many people think. Even when the prophets make reference to the future, the message is always addressed to people living at the time of the prophet. Those same predictions will speak to us today when we read the prophetic books. The significance of future predictions is meant to press upon the readers, here and now, the importance and urgency of the decisions before us. The central theme of the prophets is that God is calling His people back to Himself and the time to return is now. God sent His prophets to stir emotions and set on fire the hearts of His people for His sanctuary, His covenant, and His will.

Poetic literature: Although Job, the Psalms, and the Song of Solomon are usually categorized as wisdom literature, they are written as poems (the prophets also made free use of poetry). Of the three, only Job has a narrative beginning and end. Job is a heart-wrenching poem about the search for justice in a world where bad things happen to good people. The Psalms are primarily songs of worship that contain a wide variety of confessions, complaints, requests, and professions of faith or praises of God's great creation, His power, and His majesty. The Song of Solomon is a celebration of romantic love. It is easy to see why the themes running through these three books are best expressed in the emotionally stimulating language of poetry.

Letters: Paul's writings are referred to as "books" (e.g. The Book of Romans), but he never wrote an actual book. Paul wrote letters. There are letters in several historical books also (e.g., 2 Kings and Ezra). However, the New Testament does have entire letters from beginning to end. The letters, of course, are only one side of a two-way conversation.

It seems that I cannot keep myself from listening to my wife when she talks to someone on the phone. When I try to figure out what they are discussing by hearing only what my wife says, I get certain assumptions and then I often interrupt her with my opinions. Nine times out of ten, my wife politely informs me that I am way off the mark. In a similar way, this is what we have to do with the biblical letters. Knowing something about the historical and cultural situations of the cities where the letters were written and where they were received is of great value in piecing together the half of the conversation that we hear. As a rule, each letter contains enough clues to get a reasonable picture of why specific issues were addressed. Imagine what a help it would be if we knew the communication that was delivered to Paul when in 1 Corinthians 7:1 he says, "Now concerning the things about which you wrote…"

Scripture is not Written to You but for You

How did we miss fact that scripture is not written *to* us but *for* us? We forget that, like our incarnate Lord, the Scriptures are both divine and human. Many of us, through the influence of a dynamic pastor or Bible teacher, dove into the Scriptures to acquire the best possible understanding of God's word. I know many believers who have studied Bible study methods. In fact, I have taught courses on how to study the Bible, and looked carefully at the original languages, the histories and cultures of biblical times, paid close attention to context, and worked hard at forming a correct interpretation of the passage before me. After all, this is God's self-revelation and the source of Christian theology that provides us with the information we need to defend our beliefs.

There could be an unexpected problem. What we have forgotten is that the Bible was written *by* real people, *to* real people, struggling with real-life situations. The inspired authors were not thinking of us nor the sort of world that we live in today. They had other people and other concerns in mind. For example, Paul's writings are sometimes referred to as "Occasional Letters." This means that Paul addressed specific events or occasions that were relevant to his readers. The Corinthians needed to learn how to get along with each other; the Galatians needed a reminder to stay locked into grace; Timothy required instructions regarding the spiritual organization and administration of a living church; and a slave needed to be forgiven by his Christian master.

It is true that we can get lost in the specific purpose of each letter and it feels like we are reading someone else's mail. But that is merely the opposite extreme of forgetting that the Bible was not written for scholars and seminary students but for average men and women. The amazing fact remains that in spite of what the issue being addressed was at that moment in history, the God-given inspiration behind them produces a timeless revelation.

What is the healthy balance between focusing on either the divine or the human aspect of the Scriptures? Simply this: we have been so very blessed to be given a sacred text that was written to people, about people, by people, and for people. All have struggled to understand our Creator. Furthermore, God has planted the resolution to this great struggle within this sacred text. The Bible is all about God and people like us, which is the reason we can relate to them. We are able to live the missionary lifestyle because we are broken, confused at times, and we have a willing spirit embodied in weak flesh. We are burdened with imperfection yet loved and adopted by God the Father through the Son who has always wanted to bring us home, and by the power of the Spirit who "testifies with our spirit that we are children of God" (Romans 8:16).

As an example of God using imperfect people to bring about His kingdom, consider Saint Paul the Apostle. In his letter to the Philippians, Paul's emotional energy intensified as he warned the crew in Philippi of heretical "dogs" and "evil workers" who posed a threat to their faith. If they had their way, the Philippians would have lost Jesus in the process of becoming more religious. Some of those dangerous people had impressive religious credentials, but Paul argued that his credentials were just as impressive, even exceptional. He was truly Jewish, "circumcised the eighth day", and belonged to a respectable tribe. He was a "Hebrew of Hebrews," a Pharisee, a zealous persecutor, and as far as the law could take one toward righteousness, he was "blameless." Then he turned a corner and said,

> But whatever things were gain to me, those things I have counted as loss for the sake of Christ. More than that, I count all things to be loss in view of the surpassing value of knowing Christ Jesus my Lord, for whom I have suffered the loss of all things... (Philippians 3:1-8)

Paul was dictating this letter to a personal attendant who was writing it all down. Imagine him pacing the floor and waving his arms as he delivers the next line:

> I count all things to be loss in view of the surpassing value of knowing Christ Jesus my Lord, for whom I have suffered the loss of all things, and count them but *rubbish* so that I may gain Christ.

You might recall that the King James Version does not use the word "rubbish" but "dung." Which one is the most accurate translation of the Greek word *skubala*? First, this is the only time this word appears in the New Testament. Secondly, there may be some confusion as to how this word was formed. Most likely Paul blurted out a word that had the force of a vulgarity, the closest English word being s**t. It is not likely that you learned this in Sunday school, but a Greek scholar, Daniel Wallace, explains that the Apostle Paul determined to make it clear that his ultra-religious past was not only worthless ("dung or manure"), but repulsive (s**t). Wallace also points out that Paul had previously used such graphic expressions for its shock value when he referred to the "evil workers" and "the mutilation" a play on the word circumcision (vv. 2-3). According to Wallace, Paul's use of *skubala* is comparable to how it was used in other documents to give emotional force to the point being made. What does this tell us? Paul was more concerned with being a real person, and he communicated a message to real people with a relevance and force they could easily remember.

Paul's passion for Jesus Christ and the true faith of His followers was such that he had no use for propaganda nor writing what would be the equivalent of a clever bumper sticker or T-shirt slogan. The believers to whom he wrote were as human as you and me, forging their way to a life in God within a world dominated by the Roman Empire that had little or no knowledge of the God of Abraham or of Jesus Christ His Son. They were experiencing the labor pains of the kingdom of heaven straining to enter the world's cultures, not knowing for certain what that would look like or how it would affect their lives. Like grass growing through cracks in a concrete sidewalk, Paul and his followers were a tiny minority movement pushing upward through that particular godless age with a vision of the age to come.

Scripture Reveals God's Desire to Recover, Redeem, Reconcile, and Restore All Things

In 1517, when Martin Luther nailed his famous *Ninety-five Theses* to the door of the castle church in Wittenberg, Germany, his intent was not to break from Roman Catholicism but to advocate reforms in practices and policies. Eventually, one of the great concerns of the reform movement was to make the Bible available to all Christians in their own language (even Luther's *Ninety-five Theses* was written in Latin, not German). Johannes Gutenberg's invention of the printing press enabled Martin Luther's message to reach all of Europe through the many books he wrote. Luther was also able to provide Germany with a greater number of bibles that were printed more rapidly than at any other time in history, and they were translated into a vernacular that any German could easily understand.

We are on the brink of another great proliferation of the Scriptures. In our lifetime, we will see the Bible translated into all 6,500 (roughly) languages spoken in the world. Universal access to the Scriptures shares certain features with both the "confusion of tongues" in Genesis 11:1-9 and the "gift of tongues" in Acts 2:1-11. The technology today is not the printing press but that which is seen in even impoverished corners of the world—cell phones, in particular, smartphones. We will no longer be dependent on translations because people will be able to hear the Bible read in their own heart language as well as read it themselves.

It has been said that we stand on the verge of a spiritual awakening of a global scale. Why? Because all people will have access to God's Word, in which God not only presents humankind with knowledge of Himself but with insight into themselves, each other, the universe in which we live, and the flow of time up to the end. People living anywhere in the world will be able to learn how to return to God. They will experience the way He restores His original design for our individual lives and our lives together in community.

There is one other factor in this expansion of biblical truth that deserves serious thought. The Christian church may no longer be the agency for getting the Bible into the hands of every man, woman, and child as has been the rule. Nor will the church have control of who receives the Scriptures or how they are interpreted. Individuals, families, neighborhoods, villages, and cities of every nation will be able to experience God's word for themselves. Then, everyone who reads in faith and with an open heart will be restored to the life in God that our Creator had in mind before the Fall! Scripture does not give us a religious code to follow; instead, we are given a lifestyle to embrace.

The Pharisees had reduced the dynamic faith of Israel's heroes to a religious code. They had taken the Jewish law, which was relational and made it moral. That the heart of the law was relational is evident in the fact that Jesus could say:

"You shall love the Lord your God with all your heart, and with all your soul, and with all your mind. This is the great and foremost commandment. The second is like it, 'You shall love your neighbor as yourself.' On these two commandments, the whole Law and the prophets depend" (Matthew 22:37-40)

And Paul could say, "…love is the fulfillment of the law" (Romans 8:8-13).

Jesus' "new commandment" was definitely relational, "A new commandment I give to you, that you love one another, even as I have loved you, that you also love one another" (John 13:34).

As we meet Jesus Christ through the Scriptures, our stories are rewritten by His story and, in fact, rewritten into His story. We are like the man whom Jesus freed from a legion of demons. Note that when the man begged Jesus to let him travel with him, the Lord did not take him along:

> And He did not let him, but He said to him, "Go home to your people and report to them what great things the Lord has done for you, and how He had mercy on you." And he went away and began to proclaim in the Decapolis what great things Jesus had done for him; and everyone was amazed (Mark 5:19-20)

Jesus had given the man a story to tell. His life had been changed by the mercy the Lord had shown him.

Sometimes when we read biblical stories we come across something we find disturbing. If we get frustrated or turn away from the text because we do not like what it says, we will lose part of the story. It is not the Bible's job to make us feel good. Those disturbing parts were meant to be disturbing. If we stay with those passages and wrestle with them as Jacob wrestled with God, we will come to a resolution. Those passages may never be our favorites, but we may be totally at peace with them. We will have engaged our rational minds as we work through the text and surrounding passages. We will have paid attention to our emotions—how they are stirred by the text and what that means. We will have asked many questions. Some questions will have been answered by that divine intuition through which God's Spirit speaks to us. Many times, we discover that the hard passages have become more meaningful than those that are easy to read and accept.

Story Cultures

There are at least two religious traditions shaped by the Scriptures in which ninety-five percent of the next generation children continue in the faith of their parents. Those biblical religions are Judaism and Amish Christianity. After studying about Jewish and Amish homes, a friend of mine made an interesting observation. In both faiths—Judaism and Amish Christianity—great importance was placed on the family being together for dinner. Every night during mealtime, the Bible would be read. Usually, the father chose passages that are central to their faith. The family would discuss the passage, ask questions about its meaning, and individuals could answer how they felt the passage had related to them. Most children who grew up in these homes rarely experienced a crisis of faith when they got out on their own. They have learned and internalized the story.

In biblical Hebrew there was no word for "history." Today's spoken Hebrew has borrowed a Greek word for history, but in the past Israel did not have a history. Instead, God's people shared a collective memory. They did not think of past events as something other people experienced a long time ago, but as the experience of important family members. We can forget history and still function normally in family, neighborhood, and workplace. But if we lose our memory, then we forget who we are and our lives unravel. Constant immersion in the story refreshes and strengthens our memory and keeps our place in the story alive.

Let's become people of God's story. Let's go to our people and beyond with the message of the great things the Lord has done for us. Let's share our story of how God has recovered, redeemed, reconciled, and restored us. There has never been a time when so many people are overwhelmed by despair, never a time when the world needed hope more than now. We have the story of hope, personalized by Jesus into our own living story. We can know God and in knowing Him and come to know our true selves.

Is there any value in memorizing Bible verses? Of course there is! But I would challenge you to go further and learn the context of the stories by heart! Be a person who sees someone struggling but instead of tossing a memory verse at them, say, "Let me tell you a story." Then pull out one of the amazing stories from the Bible. Share the divine Word, which is able to save our souls.

five
Practice #3: Change Together

In our social world, the do it yourself (DIY) culture, the experience of togetherness, is all but lost. Recent research tells us that the new drug is people. Does that sound bizarre? In a world that is electronically hyper-connected, meeting a person for the first time has become the new narcotic. Many people of all ages have found that they cannot break their daily addiction to social media: Facebook, Instagram, LinkedIn, Twitter, and so on. If you were born in the late 1970s or early 80s, the world you entered bears little resemblance to the world today. I speak from experience.

I will never forget the first time I talked with a girl on the phone. I was in third grade when for some unknown reason the cutest girl in my class decided to call my house. You may remember a time when telephones were wired to the wall. At that time, a few "early adapters" had cordless phones, but those were still rare in our neighborhood. That day, the phone rang and Mom answered, and then she yelled, "Matty, phone call!" (Ugh! I always hated it when she called me "Matty.")

I ran down the stairs and into the living room, grabbed the phone, and in front of everyone sitting there I blurted out loudly: "Hello?"

"Hi, Matt, this is Lynn."

There was a long paused. My cheeks burned. "Uh, uh, uh, uh…" I stammered. With my family as witness to my awkwardness, my heart hammered against my rib cage and I thought I was going to pass out. Why did Lynn call me? To this day I have no idea.

The world I grew up in, you had to leave messages on machines that recorded our words on cassette tapes if no one answered the phone. I could not be certain that if I left a message for a friend that his parents would not hear it before he did. In fact, we were forced by circumstance to talk to adults. We had to learn the art of diplomacy when talking with our friends' folks to win their approval so they would let their son come out to play. It was a different world back then. If you liked a girl, you had to talk to her face-to-face or voice-to-voice. Of course, it was possible (but perilous) to pass messages in class. Teachers and other students could hack into them with no technical knowledge or skills. You could write letters, but only if the girl you liked lived far away, and if she lived far away, what was the point? Connecting to people always seemed to cost you something and required skills beyond the use of words. We spoke with facial expressions (especially our eyes), our voices (volume and intonation), our bodies (especially our hands), and by moving our heads (tilt, nod, turn away). As long as you could manage all of that, you would have a friend for sure. Few of us had the energy for more than two or three friends since communicating with them meant communicating with their families as well. We lived in a community without ever having to think about it.

Alone in a Virtual Crowd

The electronic communication of our digital age has changed all of that. Once our phones were taken off their leash to the wall, they became attached to us. We no longer need to run to the kitchen or living room to answer the phone. We can take calls from anywhere in the house or from almost anywhere our bodies go at any time of the day or night. In one way, we are more connected than at any other time in human history.

Through smartphones, computers of various shapes and sizes, and social media, we are able to share ideas, stories, and photographs in real time with people all over the world without leaving our house. Even fifty years ago this was impossible to imagine. We can communicate with more people instantly than our great-grandparents could meet within an entire lifetime. We can also learn a great deal of information about individuals without them ever knowing we are looking through their (Internet) windows. If we wish to make contact with others, we can hide our true identity and present ourselves with impersonal titles or false names and pictures of other people. It is easier than ever before to socially ambush other people, shooting at them from behind the comfort of our room with anonymous posts. Uncensored attacks on others can be so devastating that courts in the United States had to pass anti-bullying laws with specific reference to social media. It is not unusual to discover that the most outspoken and obnoxious rants online have been posted by someone, who in the presence of flesh and blood people, is socially awkward or even barely able to hold a conversation.

The irony of all this is that in spite of so much communication we are not developing real relationships with anyone. Few people grasp that whoever or whatever appears to us on a screen or through an electronic device is not a person but a media image. We try to remind ourselves of this by using the term "virtual reality," but we are gradually forgetting that, in this context, "virtual" means approximate yet artificial. Instead, we are beginning to think of it as reality but in another form. In mistaking virtual relationships for the real experience, we are missing out on life's most meaningful connections, not to mention, the essence of Christian spirituality.

Not long ago, I made a major mistake in Seoul, South Korea, by boarding a train during rush hour. After gliding underground on an escalator, I found my way to the platform where I had to wait for the subway train to arrive. When the cars pulled into the terminal, I saw that they were packed with commuters. Waiting for the doors to open, I assumed there would be a mad rush of people exiting the human-size sardine cans. No such luck. Only one woman stepped out before I, and thirty of my new BFFs, crammed ourselves through the doorway and into the crowded compartment.

Squished inside the car, I could barely breathe. I pulled on a handle above my head and was able to raise myself up enough for my lungs to expand a millimeter or two. Five minutes later, we arrived at the next stop. Wouldn't you know, one woman left the car and twenty more people boarded. I rode like this for what seemed to be the longest sixty minutes of my life.

One of the unpleasant sights I noticed during this ordeal was that the perspiration that had beaded on one man's forehead dripped onto another man's shoulder. Moreover, I am pretty sure that I was not the only person who felt someone's body pressing against parts of my body that in polite society we do not mention by their proper names.

But the strangest feature of this journey in the human cattle car was the total silence. No one spoke a word. Had there been room for a pin to drop, everyone would have heard it. But everyone was absorbed in his or her own electronic device. Each was in his or her own private zone, oblivious to the men and women so physically close. I wanted to scream, "Hey, everyone! Doesn't this seem like an awkward way to ride to and from work every day? Look at this guy sweating on that guy. Maybe he should at least introduce himself!"

How can we be so close, so connected to the world, yet so isolated from each other? And this relational distance is not unique to subway trains. It is a phenomenon that has influenced our churches and neighborhoods as well.

Aye, there's the rub.

Christianity is nothing if not a community. Why?

Because this is the nature of our God.

Fr. Romuald, OSB, a beloved monk who lived in a hermitage near Big Sur, California, once told a friend of mine, "The fundamental revelation of the Trinity is relationship. This is the nuclear core of the Athanasian Creed, reminding us, that we worship God in Trinity, and Trinity in Unity; neither confounding the Persons nor dividing the substance." The community of the church reflects the community that exists within the church's triune God.

When God made humans in His image, He created them "male and female" (Genesis 1:27; cf. Genesis 5:2). This may indicate that both sexes reflect the image of God or that both sexes are required to complete God's image in humankind. Either way, the original union of male and female (Genesis 2:24) constitute the primal structure of a community that naturally gives birth to an ever-widening society. We were made for God, but we were also made for each other. Surveying His handiwork on the sixth day of creation, "God saw all that He had made, and behold, it was very good." Well, almost all that He had made. Something was still missing. "Then the LORD God said, 'It is not good for the man to be alone'" (Genesis 2:18).

Speaking of handiwork, Paul made the remarkable statement: "We are His workmanship, created in Christ Jesus for good works, which God prepared beforehand so that we would walk in them" (Ephesians 2:10). What a complex and elegant revelation. God re-created us for a lifestyle of good works. Paul did not for a moment suggest that by our works we would earn a relationship with God. That is flatly contradicted by the context of "mercy" and "grace" in this passage and the explicit statements that these gifts come not from ourselves nor "as a result of works" (see Ephesians 2:1-10). We do not devote ourselves to helping others survive in the world or to come to know God in order to earn a relationship with God. That does not work. We are devoted to loving our neighbors as ourselves because that is the purpose of our re-creation in Jesus. It is what He created us to do.

Going a step further into the text, the Greek word that workmanship was translated from is "*poiema*" It is not difficult to see how our English word poem is derived from *poiema*. Although it would be going a bit far to define this Greek word as "masterpiece," the fact remains that God made humankind in His own image in order to fulfill His purpose in the world He created. Everyone on Earth is in various stages of God's handiwork as He molds, chips, smoothes, hammers, and purifies (through water and fire). What are the tools God uses in shaping us? Here is a key lesson about our spiritual development: it is not a do-it-yourself project. We cannot find a YouTube video that shows us how to put our souls together. Instead:

Iron sharpens iron,

So, one man sharpens another. (Proverbs 27:17)

Instead, speaking the truth in love, we are to grow up in all aspects into Him who is the head, even Christ, from whom the whole body [Christian community], being fitted and held together by what every joint supplies, according to the proper working of each individual part, causes the growth of the body for the building up of itself in love. (Ephesians 4:15-16)

A theological term that describes how God works through one human to help form the spiritual growth of another is "incarnational." This refers to the flesh and blood embodiment of His Spirit working between two people or among a group of people of twelve, fifty, one hundred, or more. As we live together in devotion to Jesus Christ, our interactions are characterized by a mutual ministry in which each of us alternates between being a receiver and a giver.

Why Love as an Abstraction is Easier than the Real Thing

Sometimes a drawback to joining a spiritual community is that our society is not only connected electronically while isolated physically, but it is also highly mobile. Employees find themselves working in Dallas, Texas, one year and in Dubai in the United Arab Emirates the next. People work from hotels and offices all over the globe. Why get to know my neighbor? Either they will be gone in a couple of years or we will be transferred to another state. Why get personal?

65

Many of us know rejection. Some of us have already been rejected by a Christian group. Perhaps we did not share their ethnicity, culture, worldview, or peculiar doctrines. We did not dress right, drive the right kind of car, or grow up as a member of their clique. Insider groups have many ways of pushing strangers to the margins. Why risk the pain of being a relational casualty of a community of closed-off Christians? Loneliness is less glaring and easier to deal with in solitude than in a crowd of cold shoulders.

Experiencing a church split can feel exactly like being the child of good parents who divorce. You have loved and trusted people on both sides of the split, but now you are told that if you talk to a McCoy you are disloyal to the Hatfields, and if you sympathize with the Hatfields you are not allowed to fellowship with the McCoys. Church splits are typically confusing, chaotic, and warlike. For those who did not see it coming or chose not to take sides, it can feel like their hearts have been ripped out of their bodies. Many of them never again risk setting foot in another church.

Most every relationship, whether with an individual or a group, passes through a romance stage into a now-I-know-you-better stage when all the weird stuff begins to rise to the surface. But if we bolt from a relationship the moment we see another person's humanity, we will never reach the next stages of humility, acceptance, integrity, and eventually togetherness. Sadly, while crying out to Jesus to change us, we avoid the very means He provides to grow into full maturity in Him. A mature relationship with Jesus requires forming and living in mature relationships with others. Restore us, oh Lord!

Do you want to be restored? Then round up your friends, commit your lives to the one center of the universe, Jesus Christ, and grow closer to each other as you grow closer to Him. And when the going gets tough... stay. Love and forgive. Love and reconcile. Love and accept. If you must speak the truth, wait until you have mastered the art of speaking the truth in love.

A Plan to Change the World

If you were assigned the task of creating an international organization dedicated to turning worldwide public opinion toward God, would you spend roughly three years training eleven young men (not one of whom held a degree in theology, marketing, or who had no formal education), then delegate the project to them and leave it in their hands to complete? I would not. But Jesus did. Although Jesus had every material and divine resource at His disposal, He chose to work through people. That Christianity is still around today. It has an undeniable positive influence throughout the world.

But why did it work? Because God unleashed the power of His Spirit into men and women who were of the same mind and bound together in prayer (Acts 1:14; 2:1-4). Paul understood this social dynamic of the Spirit even though he had spent much time alone. He knew that his ministry would not have been possible without his "fellow workers" (Greek: *synergos*; e.g., Romans 16:3; 1 Corinthians 3:9; Philippians 4:3; etc.). God's Spirit honors the "together" factor of Christian service and by togetherness unleashes the synergy that produces change. This is true regardless of whether we are talking about change that is occurring worldwide, in our neighborhoods, or even in our own personal lives. The "where two or three agree" rule still applies (Matthew 18:18-19).

The famous saying, "It is lonely at the top," is no doubt

true in political, corporate, educational, and even religious institutions. But the inverted model of Jesus Christ places "the greatest" beneath everyone else, supporting and serving those around and above them. Those whom Jesus calls to the lowest place are never lonely, for He sends them out in pairs, and as they go forward in His will, He gives them "brothers and sisters and mothers and children" (see Luke 10:1 and Mark 10:30). Make no mistake, the lonely superhero who stands apart from others, needing no one's help, is a myth. When people strive to attain that image, it might be that behind the mask there lurks a narcissist. "But it is not this way among you," Jesus said to His disciples, and then set them to the task of serving, even as He did not come to be served, but to serve (Mark 10:42-45). His disciples became His circle of friends, and those friends became a community. Members of that community traveled together. Even when Peter boldly proclaimed the gospel on the "day of Pentecost," He was not alone, for the eleven were right there with Him (Acts 2:14). The call of Jesus is about moving together, about the covenant community, about the heavenly family, missional brothers, or whatever else you choose to call it.

Do you want to be radical?

Do you want to change the world?

Do you want to fight injustice? Ignite revival?

If so, start with a commitment to being friends with other disciples, an active member within a spiritual community, a brother or sister to your Christian siblings. Decide that you are going to stand at their side through thick and thin. Risk venturing into deep places with a couple of friends. Spur each other on to become God's workmanship. Experience restoration through fellowship. Discover what God is doing in your corner of the world, jump in, and do the work with the others. In this hyper-connected age, ravaged as it is by loneliness, form a group that sets a table and invites those who live isolated lives on the margins of society to come and be refreshed in God's love.

Will doing these things earn you spotlight time on a stage? Will it put you in front of the cameras? Probably not. We return to the old ways of Jesus, and like Him, we risk being called "a friend of sinners" because we receive them and eat with them. We need to stop acting like a handful of evangelists and nuns who are supposed to be the representatives of Christendom and by themselves actively love the world's outcasts, invalids, and sinners. There are enough of us in this heavenly orchard, and if we all bore fruit, everyone on the planet could soon know the truth of God in Christ. Like my friend, Noah, says, "We can wrap this whole thing up and head home if we all just reach out with our hands and grab others!" Remember that change only happens together.

six
Practice #4: Shape Culture

Like most baby boomers, my mom can tell you exactly where she was and what she was doing the moment she learned that President John F. Kennedy had been assassinated on November 22, 1963. Her recollection and description of it was so vivid that I grew up feeling like I had been there myself. It was an event that marked her generation. My generation has also been marked by the shock, grief, and outrage of an event imprinted on our collective memory. We are still haunted by images from that dreadful morning, September 11, 2001.

September 10, 2001: I arrived home late at night after a long flight from New York to Hawaii, so I went to bed and passed out. A couple of hours later I was awakened and forced out of bed by the incessant ringing of my phone. My mother's panicked voice yelled, "Matthew, we're being bombed, we're being bombed!" In a slightly delirious state, I ran into my living room, stumbled around in the dark, and turned on the television. At first my mind could not comprehend the horror.

September 11, 2001: Many friends joined me that entire day, frozen in front of the television screen, overwhelmed by what we were watching. The whole nation was trying to make sense of the brutal assault. Later on, the "lucky ones," who had overslept that morning or for some other reason were spared death that day, found themselves in therapy to overcome survivor's guilt. Thousands of people died that day. Some of them were friends of people I knew, and their deaths left their families without financial support. Perhaps the most heartbreaking were the children who were orphaned instantly. While the Twin Towers may have been symbolic of the modern western world to sociopathic terrorists, they were just workspaces for thousands of beloved men, women, and children.

May 2, 2011: I was multitasking, scrolling through my Facebook messages while talking on the phone. Someone posted a message that was quickly followed by dozens more—a nationwide sigh of relief and affirmation of justice served. "Osama bin Laden has been killed." Almost every other status update had something to say about his much deserved "execution." Initially, it seemed too good to be true. *Did we really find him? Was he not able to slip away this time? Is it true that he is dead?* But then my second reaction surprised even me. Many of my friends posted comments of celebration, like a victory lap or dancing in the end zone. I understood the anguish that evoked an outcry for justice, which for many had morphed into a sort of patriotic demand for vengeance. But the way that some Christians engaged in the jubilation made me feel uncomfortable. I also felt conflicted and perplexed. No question, Bin Laden was an evil person, a murderer and calculated mastermind of the deadliest act of terror on American soil. If anyone ever deserved capital punishment, Osama bin Laden was certainly a prime candidate. But was he not, like every other human, made in God's image? Was he not a lost son, as the Prodigal was a lost son, and as I was prior to coming to faith? Was he given the opportunity to hear the truth of God in Jesus Christ before he died? Should this not be a concern of all Christians for all people?

Why concern ourselves with these sorts of questions? After all, the bad guy died, the good guys won, end of story. What disturbed me was something I read in the prophecy of Micah:

He has shown you, O man, what is good;
And what does the LORD require of you
But to do justly…
So far so good, right? But consider what comes next:
To love mercy,
And to walk humbly with your God? (Micah 6:8, NKJV)

When it comes to our enemies, whether national or personal, we get stuck when it comes to the second and third part of what God requires. But to understand and know God means, in part, is to understand that He is "the LORD, exercising lovingkindness [mercy], judgment, and righteousness in the earth," and that He "delights in mercy," preferring it over sacrifice (Jeremiah 9:23-24; Micah 7:18; Hosea 6:6).

The Transcendent Kingdom

There is much about the kingdom of God that is unlike any conceivable human society. For example, paradox seems to play an important role in God's kingdom—to keep your life you must lose it; to be first you must be last; if someone slaps you in the face, you offer them the other cheek as well. The Beatitudes, in fact, lead us in the opposite direction from the values of most nations of the earth. John Stott, a well-known Christian theologian, wrote a book, *Christian Counter Culture* about the Sermon on the Mount. When we begin to inhabit the teaching of Jesus, we discover the radical tension between God's kingdom and our native soil. Unfortunately, the closest many of us ever get to the kingdom of God is when we learn about it in Bible studies. The rest of the time, we follow the same paths and patterns as the rest of the world.

Listen to the conversations or read the posts of most of vocal believers and you get the impression that being a Christian consists of not using profanities, not drinking alcoholic beverages, not having sex outside of marriage, and quoting scripture to pass judgment on the beliefs and behavior of everyone who does not share your opinion, religious or otherwise. Woe to the person who dares to risk loving people a Christian is "not supposed" to love—the homosexual, the drug dealer, employees at the abortion clinic, etc. And where did we get the idea that passing out evangelistic booklets, wearing our witness on a Jesus T-shirt with clever slogans, or threatening people with hell if they reject our elevator speech for God is the way to stand for truth or advance the kingdom of God? Although I do not consider any of these things wrong, I do see them as impatient and at times personal ego-building expressions of Jesus' mission.

Jesus' life and message were radical, so much so that His rejection was predictable. He did not walk contrary to His culture to get attention, but because the flow of society was carrying everyone further from God rather than to Him. If His contemporaries thought Jesus was moving in the wrong direction, it was because they were walking backward. The Lord's message was outside the box because it was creative, literally a new people for God and a new way of living in God. The way of the "new commandment."

Indigenous people suffer today at the merciless hands of a few military generals who have decimated villages, enslaved thousands of men and women, massacred entire communities, and committed countless atrocities. In Asia, the country of Burma is in distress. The military government changed Burma's name to Myanmar, but the United States refuses to recognize this name because of the Burmese government's false pretenses of democracy and the many human rights violations. The survival of entire people groups in Burma is threatened as army units move through the mountains, raiding one village after another.

Villagers who survive these assaults by running for shelter in the jungle are often permanently separated from their families. Children, who have witnessed the brutal rape of mothers and sisters and the murder of their parents, travel in groups throughout the mine-infested borders, seeking whatever food or refuge in Thailand. Tens of thousands of orphans live in refugee camps and their stories are just appalling and heartbreaking (estimates of orphans in Thai refugee camps range between 180,000 and 225,000 children).

Though Thailand is reluctant to admit it, such refugee camps exist. Some compounds provide shelter for as many as 58,000 people. Wedged into small areas of the jungle, there is little hope that anyone now living in the squalor of these camps will ever leave. Burma wants them only as slaves, prostitutes, or corpses. Thailand does not want them coming into their cities and villages, so they are not permitted to leave the camps. The refugees have no citizenship, and no one is fighting for their release. Nongovernmental organizations (NGOs) have provided rations of food for them but offer little help beyond that.

Everyone in the camps, whether child or adult, has spent many nights in forty-degree Fahrenheit weather with nothing more than threadbare clothes or a thin sheet to cover them. They make houses for themselves from bamboo with leaf-thatched roofs, but the feeling of death permeates the camps. The stench is not only of physical death but the death of pride and the will to live.

Despite the great loss, sorrow, and hopelessness that refugees bring with them to the camps, there are a few bright lights. One of these undaunted heroes committed to improving their situation is Dr. Simon or Pastor Simon, as he is affectionately known to his students. I enjoyed the great privilege of staying for two weeks at his seminary campus located in one of the refugee camps. Pastor Simon and his family could have lived in the safety of the Philippines where he was studying, but he chose instead to live among his own displaced people. Pastor Simon, with his parents, his wife, children, and in-laws, had walked endless, fear-fear filled days through the jungles on their way to Thailand. During the day, they used mosquito nets to catch fish, and they slept under the nets at night. They built a home for themselves as soon as they had arrived in the camp, then went to work ministering to the spiritual needs of the refugees.

While visiting, I adopted Karen-style clothing and names to better identify with the Karen nationals of Burma. This also helped open the hearts of those in the camp to our presence. Since foreigners are not allowed to stay in the camps for long, I would not leave the camp until I had completed two weeks of teaching.

Pastor Simon works in his camp with a Christian seminary that has an enrollment of approximately five hundred students. Some have risked their lives to escape a camp to come and study in his school. Most of the professors fly to Thailand from Nagaland in India and teach up to three months at a time. Unlike the rest of the camp, the seminary is a place that vibrates with life, hope, and lots of laughter. The two weeks that I taught gave me many unforgettable experiences, but there was one in particular that stands out.

On the first day of the second week of our course on inductive Bible study methods, I was passing out materials to assist the students in our practical application "lab" time. I asked if anyone had questions before we got underway. In my pride I thought I could answer any question. Never could I have anticipated the first question raised, nor could I have prepared myself to give an answer.

The questioner was petite. There was nothing in her appearance to make her stand out, and I cannot remember seeing her again after the day she posed her question. "Is it okay," she asked, "for a pastor to defend his church when the Burmese soldiers come into our village? Does God allow us to kill them like they kill us?" She was not asking about a just war in a theoretical context. She was not describing a hypothetical situation. In that moment, I questioned whether I should tell her to turn the other cheek, to love her enemies. Who knew how many innocent villagers were dying in the jungles while I was hesitating during that intense silence.

A young man named Lehtie stood up and politely asked if he could answer that question. I thought, *Hurray! I'm rescued.* Lehtie turned to the young woman and said, "No, we are not to fight."

Are you kidding me? I was shocked. *Those Burman soldiers will destroy you and your family.* It's not a matter of killing but of defending. Lettie continued, "We are not fighting for a kingdom here on Earth. We are free. We are free because we fight for a kingdom that is not of this world." He grabbed the flesh of his skinny arm and said, "They can beat, hurt, and kill this. They can hold us in this camp, but they cannot take what is in our hearts. And because of that, we are free."

Heads nodded in agreement as Lehtie sat down. They understood what he was saying. They were at peace. No arguments or debates, just peace. From then on, I noticed the pervasiveness of peace, that it was everywhere throughout their camp. Peace, when they told their stories of horror; peace, when they awoke at four in the morning to cook their rations; peace, when the rain and humidity of the dense forest mildewed their clothes and ruined their homes. They were free.

When we have a perspective like Lehtie's, it changes everything. We are not waiting until heaven to become perfect in our love for all those whom God loves. We do not find it impossible to give away our possessions, our time, our energy to bring food, shelter, or life to others. We can be generous with what we have because we are going to let go of it all day when we cross the threshold of eternity. Our accounts are short term, our hearts are not anchored to geography, our words are those of Christ, and His words are life. We believe the best for others and that it is God's will we work to that end. We believe it is possible to live in a manner that has people asking what it is that enables us to share so much truth, goodness, and beauty. We believe we truly are the salt of the earth and the light of the world. That is how we brighten and change the world around us.

Has Social Justice Become a Distraction?

You may be ready to stone me for even posing the question, "Has social justice become a distraction?" but you would have to know my history, which has brought me around to asking such a thing. I have spent the better part of a decade sharing the gospel in practical ways. I have participated in founding injustice awareness movements, worked with friends to provide technologies for clean water and sustainable food in remote areas, taught people around the world how to document and report instances of injustice, and built homes for homeless.

I was prodded to rethink the priority of all of these activities one day when a friend Len challenged my concept of "missions" and helped me see how it looks side-by-side with Jesus' life mission.

Len: "Matt."

Me: "Yeah?"

Len: "When you stand before Jesus at the end of your life, what will you ask for, justice or mercy?

Me: "Uh, mercy."

Len: "Matt."

Me: "Yes, Len?"

Len: "What was one of the biggest injustice issues of Jesus' day?"

Me: "Slavery?"

Len: "Yes. And when did Jesus talk about the justice of fighting to free slaves?"

Me: "Huh?"

It was only a short conversation, but it stirred me to give it more thought.

Just for the record, I would never argue against Christians working to promote justice. In the Bible, justice is one of three ways that God commands His people to manage their social relations and interactions; the other two are righteousness and mercy. We cannot ignore instances of injustice and simply go on our way any more than Jesus could resist healing a man's hand or a woman's back on the Sabbath.

But Jesus had some surprising ideas about justice and mercy. For example, no system in first-century Israel was more subject to abuse than taxation. We can assume Jesus was concerned for people who suffered at the hands of unscrupulous people who managed this system. But He was at least equally concerned for the tax collectors. He could tell His disciples to love their enemies because He had no enemies. Every person He saw was a lost child of God and entire crowds were to Him "like sheep without a shepherd." Even in Gethsemane when face to face with Judas, Jesus addressed him as "friend." I heard someone say that orthodoxy is paradoxy. Jesus died for the oppressed and the oppressor. It is not difficult to accept the former, but it's very challenging to believe the latter. Jesus came to call to repentance:

The sexually harassed employee and the offending employer.

The guilt-ridden sinner and the self-righteous accuser.

The weary slave and the brutal master.

The oppressed worker and the narcissistic dictator.

The trafficked young woman and the perverse trafficker.

Please hear me. My blood boils when I become aware of yet another young woman or child being forced into the sex trade where their imprisoned bodies are rented to adults with vile intentions. Nor is the Bible silent regarding these offenses against human commodities and their God (cf. Joel 3:3; Revelation 18:13). How can we justify ourselves for doing nothing when it is so easy to partner with organizations that are dedicated to liberating sex slaves? But my heart is also agitated when Christians do nothing about the billions of people who never hear from us the message of hope and restoration. These people are our coworkers, people we see every day, and they don't hear our message because we are not using our voice.

In the gospels, especially in Luke, Jesus demonstrates considerable concern for the poor, the widow, the child, those who were the weakest and most vulnerable in society. But He wanted His "friends" and followers to be less concerned about "those who kill the body and after that have no more that they can do" than for "the One who, after He has killed, has authority to cast into hell" (Luke 12:4-5). The work He passed on to His apostles was less focused on liberating the oppressed but on freeing souls oppressed by the devil (Luke 13:16; Acts 10:38).

The fight for universal justice is an extremely difficult and discouraging challenge, and loving mercy and wanting to extend it to all people is virtually impossible. But things that are impossible for us are not impossible with God, "for all things are possible with God" (Mark 10:27). Loving mercy may be counter-cultural, but imagine one billion Christians waking up tomorrow and deciding they were going to practice mercy. Perhaps the whole world would be transformed. And all because we began by:

Loving mercy for our enemy;
Loving mercy for the terrorist;
Loving mercy for the rapist;
Loving mercy for the pedophile.

I know how difficult this is to imagine. Nevertheless, it may be just the place to begin. If we can learn to love mercy for the most morally unlovable people in the world, then loving mercy for everyone else will come easily. After all, Jesus Christ "who knew no sin" became sin on our behalf—the one innocent man died for the great mass of sinful humanity—"so that we might become the righteousness of God in Him" (2 Corinthians 5:21) on the cross for the guilty. That was mercy, not justice. That is the way of God and the way of our Lord, "mercy triumphs over judgment" (James 2:13).

Can you get on board with loving mercy? What I am suggesting is that rather than making awkward and inept attempts to take a stand for the truth, we devote ourselves to living the truth. It is not as though everything we have done up until now was no good, but that we exhausted precious resources majoring in minors and vice versa. The weightier issues, such as "justice and mercy and faithfulness" are the things we "should have done without neglecting the others" (Matthew 23:23). This is Jesus' mission and He has simply invited us to follow Him.

The shortest book in the Bible is also one of my favorites, and that is Paul's letter to Philemon. What I love about this brief yet touching correspondence is its backstory. The letter is addressed to Philemon, a Greek name that means "affectionate." Philemon was a Christian believer who owned slaves. Paul was close enough to Philemon to know that he could be direct with him regarding a serious and sensitive issue.

One of Philemon's slaves had escaped his household and had either gone in search of Paul or else been caught and thrown into the same prison where Paul was being held (many runaway slaves would make their way to Rome and try to lose themselves in its crowded streets). That slave was Onesimus, whose name means "profitable" (or useful), a meaning that Paul used in a play on words when recommending Onesimus back to his owner (vv. 10–11).

At some point during their incarceration, Onesimus came to faith in Jesus Christ under Paul's influence. This formed a bond between them so that Paul could refer to the slave as his "child" that he had, in his words, "begotten in my imprisonment." This statement, along with the case Paul made for Onesimus, revealed the closeness of their relationship.

In the Roman Empire of Paul's time, slavery was not one specific category but included a variety of possibilities from the bond-slave to domestic servants to stewards (who, for example, could manage a household and the personal affairs of the head of the house) to those who held "career positions," such as lawyers and sea captains. A large percentage of society was born into slavery and never knew any other way of life. Although there were the rare benevolent masters, most slaves suffered throughout their hard and precarious lives as being the subject to the whims and abuse of their owners. There were severe penalties for a slave who was guilty of a breach of contract. Fines could be imposed on anyone who offered sanctuary to a runaway slave equal to the loss a slave owner would sustain for the number of days the slave had been sheltered.

In Paul's short letter, we are provided with a real-life example of how God's transcendent kingdom entered human culture to transform it. Paul set out to reconcile a slave to his master and the master to his slave. Philemon could have beaten Onesimus, turned him over to the authorities, had him branded or put to death. Instead, Paul challenged him to do was unheard of: he'd forgiven Onesimus and received him as a "brother." In fact, you might want to return to Philemon, and as you scan through it, notice how many times Paul uses the word "brother." Timothy is "our brother," Philemon is Paul's brother, and Onesimus had become a "beloved brother" to both Paul and Philemon. Paul imagined what the kingdom of God would look like in this delicate situation. What he came up with was transformed relationships that could spread out to others and eventually transform the culture.

We cannot say for certain what became of Onesimus, but

in religious tradition, he became a bishop. At any rate, Paul was able to commend him to the Colossians as a "beloved brother" who was a reliable messenger in sharing with them Paul's circumstances (Colossians 4:7-9).

Made in the image of our Creator, we have been enlisted by God to participate with Him in the re-creation of our world. In Christ, all of us have become God's new creation. What is true of His people will become true of the cultures they inhabit and influence.

What do I mean by "culture"? I am simply referring to the ways that societies organize themselves, honoring what they perceive as the highest values, and prohibiting behavior that runs contrary to those values. Language, traditions, technology, art, and religion are a few of the primary concerns around which cultures are formed.

In 2008, an article appeared in Christianity Today in which Andy Crouch urged Christians to leave their mark on their cultures. He began with a list of positions that Christians have taken toward culture, including:

> *Condemning* Culture: looking down upon it and withdrawing from it.
>
> *Critiquing* Culture: thinking through it and discerning what is wrong.
>
> *Copying* Culture: making "Christian" versions of it, becoming what Francis Schaeffer referred to as "an echo of the world."
>
> *Consuming* Culture: just eating it up; allowing it to shape our lives.

Crouch called for a more humane mandate for moving into the future by challenging Christians to "create culture."

Does that make as much sense to you as it does to me?

We know that a person is capable of creating amazing things. How much more is a person capable of when we use these gifts in the inspiration and power of the Holy Spirit? Do not start saying, "Well, I'm not creative," because you are! Perhaps you do not paint landscapes, compose music, or write poetry, but give it some thought and you will realize that you have your own way of doing certain things that you did not learn from anyone else. We are all sculptors, using the materials that come into our hands every day to give shape to our world.

Imagine that Paul meant for us to take literally what he said about the "fruit of the Spirit"; that they are, in fact, byproducts of God's Spirit indwelling us (Galatians 5:22–23). Can you envision what it would be like if we began a daily practice to bring mindfulness to those qualities until they found a home in our inner lives? Can you see how their influence over our thoughts and actions would increase day after day? What would happen? I will tell you what I see: by becoming people who daily produced the fruit of the Spirit, we would bring a new dynamic into every environment we entered and gradually the shape of our culture would change. Our sowing to the Spirit would result in our beginning to reap life and peace.

Let us not lose heart in doing good,
for in due time we will reap if we do not grow weary.
So then, while we have opportunity,
let us do good to all people,
and especially to those who are of the household of faith.
(Galatians 6:7-10)

The values and behaviors that we learn, practice, and celebrate in our home meetings or accountability groups were never meant to be for the enhancement of our Christian communities. They are for the benefit of the culture around us.

We—who are being transformed into the image of Jesus—are also becoming agents of change in the world.

seven
Practice #5: Bless Locally

From a young age, I wanted my life to count for something. By the time I graduated high school, the most meaningful life I could imagine was to share the story of Jesus to the furthest reaches of the earth. The fact that people living in harsh or exotic places, such as Siberia and Nepal, had never heard the biblical message of Jesus in their own language was captivating to me. After years of having the privilege of serving God by serving others in such far-off places, I am still challenged by this vision. However, now I realize it is not the only mission.

Belonging to an international organization that emphasizes the practical experience young men and women gain by short-term service across cultures, my time was divided between excursions abroad and teaching and training at home in the States. As a result, I never lost my connections with friends at home even though I could spend half the year on another continent in the world. Over time, I began to realize that my friends at home were sitting at work in offices, eating in restaurants, studying in universities, and sharing apartments or neighborhood space with people who were as unaware of life in Jesus Christ as those I met in the far corners of the world. In other words, the United States had become a brand-new mission field. Western Europe is also in desperate need of hearing the truth of God in Jesus. In these "historically Christian" places, Christianity had been pushed to the margins of society. Furthermore, globalization and the arrival of the digital age had changed the face of missions forever. At that point, a red light began flashing in my mind.

Until then, my involvement with foreign missions had been in traditional Christian organizations. Now I was beginning to imagine my friends receiving the call to missions right where they lived. This grew into a vision of a new framework for non-traditional mission work around the world. Regardless of whether a believer moved into a jungle to translate the Bible into an indigenous language, providing food and water to refugee camps, or planting churches in India, these endeavors had one common purpose: to be a blessing to those who were served. My coworkers and I discovered that our mission work was a blessing, but we also realized that we were a blessing, which was a gift we could give to others around the world. The response to our service was more intense in a positive way when we engaged with others within their cultural traditions, treating them as friends and peers, and returning to visit them as many times as we possibly could.

We checked with the gospels and noticed how Jesus not only blessed people with His teaching and miracles, but He Himself was a blessing. In Paul's writings, we learn that God has blessed us with Jesus and through Jesus "blessed us with every spiritual blessing" (Ephesians 1:3). God has also passed on to the church Abraham's calling, that in him "all the nations will be blessed" (Acts 3:25; Galatians 3:8). Our attention is drawn to the supernatural signs that confirmed the apostles' preaching, the good news spreading out from Jerusalem in all directions, and the growth of the church both in Jerusalem and in the formation of new Christian communities throughout the Roman Empire. However, all of these hinged on believers being a blessing to those to whom they were sent. That is why rejoicing was a consistent response to the apostles' ministry (Acts 8:8, 39; 13:48; 16:34). People who were allegedly sent from God but were not a blessing failed to manifest the kingdom of God, which is "righteousness and peace and joy in the Holy Spirit" (Romans 14:17).

There it is, the defining idea of God's blessings being dispersed to the world through His Christian people. I do not claim that this is a new idea or new revelation, but I believe it has been confined to our churches and only rarely leaked outside its walls. The majority of my own experience has been in Evangelical churches where I have frequently heard believers talking about how they had been blessed by one another by some good touch of God's grace, or perhaps refer to another church member as "such a wonderful blessing." I do not recall hearing unbelievers talk about how blessed they were by Christians, or the perfect wave, or by a parking space close to the door of a grocery store. We do not own the word "blessing," but we have kept it to ourselves.

Have you seen the "Christian" Yellow Pages? Scroll through the ads and you will find the blessing of a Christian plumber, car dealer, insurance agent, and so on and on. Perhaps the blessing will come in the form of warm and friendly service (possibly even a moment of prayer together), a better deal, and the whole transaction handled with integrity. If you buy a new car, for instance, look for a nice Christian single mother who could use the car, and bless your old car as a gift. When we live in a community of blessings, we come to expect blessings. How could it be otherwise? "For you know the grace of our Lord Jesus Christ, that though He was rich, yet for your sake He became poor, so that you through His poverty might become rich" (2 Corinthians 8:9) and "He who did not spare His own Son, but delivered Him over for us all, how will He not also with Him freely give us all things?" (Romans 8:32).

Sometimes within our churches we enjoy an abundance of blessings in Jesus our Lord, but do we then forget to carry them home with us for the purpose of sharing them with the world? Herein lies the problem in churches that seem incapable of producing new converts. The light that shines in us must be the fullness of our blessings in Jesus that turn us into His blessing the others who don't know Jesus. This is the light that illuminates and the salt that flavors and preserves. Walking in the light means living out the blessings of God's word that shines in the darkness (Philippians 2:14-16). God placed His blessings upon humankind on the day we were created; the same word reiterated to Abraham, then pronounced by the priests of Israel, and finally being fully revealed in Jesus Christ (Genesis 1:28; Numbers 6:2-27).

Do people outside our churches hear or receive our blessings? I know for certain that they have heard our gossip and grumbling, our scandals and schisms, our complaints and condemnations. Light is most useful and shines brightest in the darkest places. Perhaps all we have done by keeping it in the sanctuary is blind ourselves to the desperate need for it to be shared with our darkened world.

You may be questioning, "But, Matt, what about finishing the great commission? What about promoting justice? What about bringing drinking water to those dying of thirst? What about taking care of widows and orphans? What about helping the foreigner?" My answer is that those are the places where the need for God's blessing is the greatest. But before we can bless others with a message, a cup of cold water, and provisions of food, clothing, and shelter, we must recognize the blessed nature of our own lives in Christ. It is the essence of what we share with those in need.

How This Looks from the Outside

When people outside of our church walls receive a blessing from us, their first reaction is to question why we would do this for them. Why is this? They assume we give as the world gives. If the world gives them something, it is expected that the world gets something in return, to obligate them, or manipulate them. In their world, no one "gives something for nothing." But we have learned from Jesus how to give blessings. For example, Jesus told His disciples, "Peace I leave with you; My peace I give to you; not as the world gives do I give to you" (John 14:27).

I recently watched a video online of a regular middle-class man who was dressed in old dirty and tattered clothes, which gave people the impression that he was homeless. He sat on the sidewalk of a busy thoroughfare and stopped people as they walked past him. Naturally, they thought he was going to ask for a handout, but instead he offered them dollar bills. The first people who encountered him had a shocking reaction. They yelled at him. They said things like, "I don't need your stinking money!" or, "You have nothing to give to me!" He was unable to bless them because they would not believe he had a blessing to give.

You see, in Jesus was life, "and the life was the Light of men," but the problem then and the problem now is that the "Light shines in the darkness, and the darkness did not comprehend it" (John 1:4-5). So that leaves us with a special type of challenge. We cannot shine a light into the faces of other people or we will blind them. This is especially so if their eyes are adjusted to the dark. Instead, we train our light on Jesus; it is our Lord that we want people to see.

We need to work with people the way Jesus worked with the blind man. After Jesus laid His hands on him, He asked: "Do you see anything?" And he looked up and said, "I see men, for I see them like trees, walking around." Then again, He laid His hands on his eyes; and he looked intently and was restored, and began to see everything clearly" (Mark 8:23-25)

So, we open the shutter just a little to allow a soft glow of yellow sunlight to enter the room. When people are able to accept that, we give them a little more light. This continues until we can feel the fullness of God's blessings burst in and illuminate His infinite grace and goodness.

There are people who live in Seattle, Washington, and are sometimes desperate for sunlight. Norwegians drink milk that is fortified with vitamin D or take supplements like melatonin to compensate for decreased sunlight. Some people suffer a form of depression during the winter months that is referred to as Seasonal Affective Disorder (SAD). Spiritually, all over the world, people are desperate for the light that is Jesus Christ and He has placed it in us so that we can share it with everyone else.

For God, who said, "Light shall shine out of darkness," is the One who has shone in our hearts to give the light of the knowledge of the glory of God in the face of Christ

(2 Corinthians 4:6).

Could we live in such a way as to become the best blessing that coworkers and customers experience in our places of employment? What if people coming to their cubicle every morning found sticky notes on their computers that encouraged them with positive expressions of truth, goodness, and beauty? What if we set out snacks on our desk two or three days a week with a small sign offering them free to anyone who needed a mid-afternoon boost of energy? What if we brought a tarp or umbrellas to soccer games to provide shade or dryness for anyone who needed it? What are other creative ways that we can be blessings to our neighbors?

It sounds easy enough, right? We treat others how we want to be treated, and we go the extra mile to brighten someone's day. So why don't we live this way? Because it is very inconvenient.

I was invited to teach in a church where I was sharing some of these ideas regarding being a blessing. During my talk, a man raised his hand and asked, "Matt, do you always bless all those around you?" Reluctantly, I was forced to admit that usually I found it too inconvenient. I told them the story of the elderly Korean woman who was struggling to carry the chair and how I didn't stop to help her. I mentioned, however, that this was a personal issue God and I were working on together. After all, that is the process of learning to become more like Jesus.

A friend of mine—also a Matt—lives in the Pacific Northwest and belongs to a family that has built homes in the area for two generations. Woodworking is his passion, and he is a talented and creative carpenter. He makes tables, chairs, couches, and even small boutique-style boxes for his clients. He is one of those very fortunate souls who has found something he loves doing and can earn a living by doing it.

One day my friend wondered what would happen if he were able to bless others by sharing his creative skills with them. He decided to take some kids from his neighborhood and give them the opportunity to shift from consumers to carpenters. He knew, however, that they would not be interested in making furniture, so he worked out a design for longboard skateboards. Word got out that he was providing free training for this craft and young men began showing up to learn from him. One of them was a seventeen-year-old who complained about how much his feet hurt from standing on them after his first day of work. Matt learned that he had spent most the summer sitting on his bed playing video games. It was the first time in weeks that he had been on his feet and was actually doing something active and productive. Since he had been blessed with a gift from my friend Matt, which was the opportunity to pour his energy into a worthwhile project, it became one of the most active periods of his life.

The young man had also become very interested in woodworking. Matt talked with the young man about creative gifts and how they are a reflection of God's creativity. This, he explained, seemed especially true in working with wood. So, over the work bench, Matt continued to disciple him, and while turning out something well-crafted, the young man became God's workmanship, created in Christ Jesus for good works.

A life of prayerful expectation causes us to become sensitive to what God is doing around us and to opportunities to join Him in His creative work. At first, we begin to notice various places where Jesus is at work on Him mission. Soon, we make these discoveries every day. Eventually, we are overwhelmed with opportunities to join God in blessing people around you.

For example: People waiting on your table in a restaurant

are desperate for encouragement or a kind word. People who ask if you can explain something are in need of direction. People who have trouble reading could use help filling out a job application. People of all ages who cannot make sense out of their lives, let alone the crazy world they bump up against every day, are in need of guidance.

Jesus touches our hearts and sends us on all of these missions, like when a conversation starts at a checkout counter and results in a stranger asking you how she can become a Christian. The blessing you have been to them during that inconvenient hour will last for eternity. All you had to do was step out of your little world for a moment and discover where God's Spirit had already been at work.

You may be thinking, "Matt, this is too simple. I actually desire to be an agent for change in the world, but this business of being a blessing seems too lame." Well, I am asking you to just give it a try. It may sound as silly as dunking yourself seven times into the Jordan River to get cured of your leprosy. Begin with an easy step. Smile at someone in the mall or in your hallway at school. Hold a door open for a stranger at a public building. When a neighbor is ill, volunteer to walk their dog. You will be shocked by the changes these little acts of kindness will make. Do this long enough and you will find that it is becoming a lifestyle.

Let me give you a dose of reality: you are not going to change the whole world. But any one of us and all of us can change a few worlds that are inhabited by friends and strangers. My friend, Eugene Cho, wrote a book titled, Overrated: Are We More In Love with the Idea of Changing the World Than Actually Changing the World? In the book, Eugene observes that people are more in love with the idea of changing the world than they are of changing themselves. Changing the world is a noble idea, but it is harmless. Changing one person's own world is doable, even if inconvenient.

I recently heard a story about Christians living in San Jacinto, California, who were outraged when a husband and wife from Los Angeles moved into town and opened an adult novelty store. Several believers from three different churches formed a small group to protest outside the store with picket signs. They had no way of knowing how many potential customers they had actually deterred, but they certain that some people had been steered away from the doors of the store. They continued their campaign for several weeks.

One person who continued to visit the store a couple of times each week was undaunted by the crowd as he politely pushed his way through the protestors. The first time Don showed up, he was carrying a mop, bucket, and other cleaning supplies. Ignoring the rebukes of the indignant Christians outside, he went to the counter and asked to speak to the manager.

"What is it you're looking for?" the manager said.

Don answered, "I want your permission to clean the bathrooms."

Surprised and wary, she said, "Why would you want to do that?"

He told her, "It's something that I do well, and knowing this part of town like I do, I can imagine they'll need a good scrubbing." Smiling, but still suspicious, she gave him permission to enter the restrooms and clean them.

Each time Don showed up, he would quietly make his way through the picket line, enter the store, and get to work on cleaning the mirrors, sinks, floors, and so on. He exchanged greetings with the woman who worked there and met her husband, but their conversations never got beyond, "How are you today?" and, "What do you think about this weather?"

One morning, the woman's curiosity got the better of her and she asked, "Don, whatever gave you the idea to come here and offer to clean our restrooms? Is this something you do for every small business in town?"

Don smiled and said, "No, I only do this for your store. Actually, the idea came to me before you opened shop. Like the others outside, I was concerned about the sort of influence this kind of store would have on our community. While I was praying about your store, I got the feeling that Jesus was telling me to come serve you. The only thing I could think of that I would be comfortable doing was washing down the restrooms."

For a moment, the woman stood there in stunned silence. Then she called out to her husband who emerged from the back room and asked Don to tell him what he had just told her. When he repeated the reason why he was there, both the husband and wife asked many questions, and Don spent a considerable amount of time talking with them about Jesus and what the Lord meant to him.

He was a blessing not a burden.

Any measurable effect we have on others will be seen in the blessing that their lives become. The movement goes outward from the One who was "the true Light which, coming into the world, enlightens every man" (John 1:9). He lifted His hands and blessed the lives of many. Each one of those who were blessed would touch others with the blessing. A life of blessing that is "fruitful and multiplies."

"Then God said, 'Let there be light'; and there was light" (Genesis 1:3).

eight
Practice #6: Engage Globally

Having spent my adult life in cross-cultural ministry as well as training others for missionary work, I have frequently been approached by people who want to know how they can get involved in overseas missions. Generally, those who ask are excited about where they would like to go and they are eager to get started. One of the first questions I ask is something like, "Where do you believe God wants you to go?" Many times, the conversation from that point has gone something like this:

"I believe God has called me to Africa, and I am very excited about having the opportunity to go there."

Sharing their excitement with perhaps the same light in my eyes, I say, "Great! Where in Africa?"

"Well, yes, like I said, I want to go to Africa."

"Good. And what country in Africa, exactly?"

"Oh, my heart is so burdened for the people of Africa

that I just want to go there."

I smile and say, "Good for you. I'd love to see photos of the country of Africa when you return."

"Okay, I'll make sure to post them on Facebook."

Perhaps that is how a lot of Christians imagine what it is to be a missionary. They feel the great spiritual need and they want to share a personal involvement. But they have only a general idea of what is actually out there in terms of men, women, and children in those faraway places. They have made very little effort to know the daily lives of the people, their geography, climate, their culture or conditions, their politics or beliefs, etc. They are more concerned about the burden they feel for "the lost" doing something heroic for the Lord, or making a statement that they care for people. We have no clue that the shirts and shoes we buy may contribute to the pain and suffering of those who need to hear about the love of God in Christ.

This is not a criticism or complaint. Something is better than nothing. There are Christians who want to share the life they have in God with others. They have come to realize that they are not the only people on Earth and ours is not the only nation. Truly we live in a smaller world than ever before, and we are more connected to that world than ever before. We have availability to more information about that world than ever before. With this greater awareness, we feel a greater responsibility and desire to do something about it.

But how do we get beyond all the ambitions, activities, and issues of our own culture to engage globally and become effective servants of Christ in other cultures?

Here is what friends have taught me about engaging globally:

A few years ago, it was Thanksgiving Day and I was resting

in the afternoon. I decided to watch a video that a friend loaned to me. (My friend knew this was exactly the sort of documentary I love to see.) The video is not a Christian production, but rather a story from the life of JJ Yemma and the work he started in Nicaragua. Yemma is a professional surfer who was drawn to the waves down south . . . way south. He describes the first time he arrived at a pristine beach in Nicaragua. There were no footprints in the sand. That Central American nation had recently emerged from Civil War and the beaches were deserted. Yemma found it so inviting, and he thought to himself, *Why don't I build a surf lodge in this beautiful spot and live here?* And that was what he did.

Sometime later, Yemma met Jesus Christ, who transformed his life. He decided to turn his lodge into a place for mission activities. He opened his doors to the people of Nicaragua and also to surfers who descended on Nicaragua for its world-class breaks. In my opinion, that is a winning combination: surf the waves, serve the Lord.

Few documentaries have affected me like Yemma's story. The natural way that his new faith in God expressed itself into his real-life situation was exactly the vision I was pursuing and trying to help others to catch. Yemma knew exactly what surfers hoped to find when they came to his lodge. He knew their language. He knew what they desired. And he knew the empty place in their soul. God uses one candle to light another.

Watching Yemma's mission unfold inspired me to exercise that kind of creativity. I imagined using the time off from work that my friends and I had for the next Thanksgiving holidays and taking perhaps a couple more days of vacation time to make an excursion to Nicaragua. While there, we would surf our brains out and serve our hearts out. When I mentioned the plan to the friends who came to mind, they immediately signed on. Besides the money that we kicked in, we were able to raise an additional $3,000 that would be used to build a brick home. All of us were amazed by what we experienced. With our vacation time, our hard-earned money, and our own hands we were able to serve the needs of a poor community and enjoy our favorite pastime doing it. We were not missionaries, at least not in the traditional sense. We were not "sent out" by a church or religious organization. We were just a few friends who had a heart to do something of value for others in the name of Jesus.

That first year of building a brick home in Nicaragua turned out to be merely the first trip of many that would follow. We celebrated Thanksgiving by taking it beyond our North American society and giving others a reason to be thankful. One couple, of the first crew to go on this venture, have purchased homes in Nicaragua and others still return every year. Lifestyle Missionaries can engage globally while staying engaged locally.

What if every able-bodied believer decided to engage globally in that manner, using the resources that are already in our hands—our skills, our hobbies, our friendships, our vacations— and found a place to refresh our hearts, renew our minds, and revive the hopes of others by providing some kind of service to them in the name of Jesus?

God to Moses: "What is that in your hand?"

Moses, "A staff." (He had carried it around in the hills for forty years, herding sheep.)

God showed Moses how to use his staff to liberate Israel.

God to Yemma, "What is that under your feet?"

Yemma, "My surfboard."

God showed Yemma how to use surfing to shape a new ministry in Central America that inspired and produced other ministries.

A friend of mine, Eugene Cho, visited a refugee camp in Thailand where he observed teachers who were working long, hard hours for meager wages to educate the children. Unable to shake the images of poor learning environments and poverty out of his head, he created a website where people could donate a day's wages to a specific cause that would benefit these people. Calculating small acts like this, multiplied by thousands of people, could help the suffering of millions of people and "alleviate extreme global poverty."

Eugene and his wife and children spent three years simplifying their lives and saving up money so that they could commit his entire salary for 2009 to that cause. That was the beginning of One Day's Wages (onedayswages.org/founders-story/), which in its first four years of operation was able to raise and give over one million dollars to great projects all around the world. Eugene and his wife were not missionaries. They did not move to a foreign country. But now they are assisting those who care for the poor, not to create in them a dependence on charity, but by empowering them to thrive and begin to set aside their own one day's wage to help others. Eugene and his family applied what they knew about the power of technology to create a platform for all believers to engage globally.

Another friend built a website that uses a simple format to lay out the basic message of how God shares His life with us through Jesus Christ. The site can be accessed any time of the day from anywhere in the world. The first website has now become a number of related sites that tell the same message in different languages. By purchasing ad space on the Google search engine, they are now seeing over a million viewers every day turn to Jesus to receive God's grace and mercy. Several hundred thousand people every day click their way through discipleship sites, and thousands have provided their email addresses so that Christians can establish contact with them to answer questions and take requests for prayer.

I have had the privilege of visiting different countries and meeting people who have come to faith through this site. Their stories are incredibly encouraging. I had a personal dialogue in Mexico City with Juan where he said, "I was in a desperate condition. I went to Google looking for stories of encouragement. As I scrolled through the websites that were listed, this one sounded like what I was hoping to find. As I read through it, I read about Jesus Christ for the first time. I gave my life to Jesus and soon someone contacted me. I was directed to a pastor nearby and in his church I am learning about the Bible. Now I am sitting here talking with you and getting the help I need."

Fifty years ago, a century ago, a millennium ago missionaries would have given God endless praise and thanksgiving if they had known that one day there would be a tool like the Internet to send the truth around the world from one's home. Missionaries are staying in contact with new converts to strengthen and deepen their faith every day. In fact, people can hear about Jesus even though they live under governments that have closed off contact with those who would carry the Christian message inside their borders. Many of today's busiest and most productive missionaries are at their computers training someone, counseling someone, or praying with someone who has been recently introduced to Jesus. This wonderful movement today is because believers decided to use the means they had to engage globally not just locally.

We can be among the first responders when a significant global event occurs and resources need to be gathered, shipped, and delivered to people in need. You may ask, "But, Matt, why should I care or get involved?" The answer is simple: because you can! Just knowing that we are not helpless, that we can announce, explain, inform, and be a link in the electronic bucket brigade is enough to stoke our compassion and unleash the mercy God has worked into our hearts.

There are those who engage globally and there are those who engage locally. Both of fine and admirable. We can tell ourselves that those who engage globally are not normal "every day" people. Meaning, they have a unique personality and situation that makes them wired to do such things. The truth is, if they had never attempted something extraordinary, their reach could have been very limited as well. When they decided that doing something for others was worth the cost and the risk, they became extraordinary. To engage globally is not based on a personality type but on the willingness to take a risk.

To be honest we do not know what we are capable of doing. We do not know what God is capable of doing through us. If you knew that investing two hours a month to communicate with one impoverished person who lives on the other side of the world would change his or her life, would you take the time to do it? What if that person became a follower of Jesus Christ simply because you showed them love and concern in His name? How could we not devote those hours to someone? It seems to me that when there is a crisis anywhere in the world in which local resources are insufficient to meet the need, Christians should be there in person or in supplies.

In the times we live in today, with information at our fingertips, it does not take much effort to find out where people are suffering because they lack the means to meet their basic human needs, or where there are refugee camps, or even where Christians are being persecuted and murdered. Thanks to the

Internet and the ubiquitous smartphones, there are few borders in the world that we cannot cross electronically. We can learn who needs help, we can communicate with those who have needs, and we can do something, perhaps just one thing, to ease the burden.

You may be asking, "Why should I be worried about what is happening to someone I do not know who lives ten thousand miles away?"

Okay, I will tell you why…

We belong to a global family, and Jesus told us to go to the uttermost parts of the earth.

Some of us already know we are members of a global family with our brothers and sisters spread all over the planet. Others do not yet realize our connection with our global neighbors. Are we going to be like Cain who refused to accept his role as his "brother's keeper"? (Genesis 4:9) What motivates us to engage globally is based on the relationship God has created between us and everyone else. The starving woman on the other side of the world could be our mother; her diseased and dying baby could be our child.

A host of scriptures come to mind regarding the love of God and how it shapes the Christian's attitude and behavior, but two seem especially relevant for our time from the books of Hebrews and Proverbs:

> Remember the prisoners as if chained with them—those who are mistreated—since you yourselves are in the body also. (Hebrews 13:3)
>
> Deliver those who are being taken away to death,
> And those who are staggering to slaughter, Oh hold them back.
> If you say, "See, we did not know this,"
> Does not He consider it who weighs the hearts?

And does He not know it who keeps your soul?

And will He not render to man according to his work?

(Proverbs 24:11-12)

The first verse, Hebrews 13:3, has to do with persecuted Christians, we might as well add anyone who is seeking peace and the welfare of others regardless of their religion or whether they even belong to a religious body. We are to identify with them, intercede for them, and affirm our solidarity with them. The second passage, Proverbs 24:11-12, addresses known instances of refugees, people suffering under oppressive governments, and groups that are targeted for ethnic cleansing. In current times, Western civilization does not permit us to fake ignorance about people under such circumstances.

It is not my job to tell you how to feel about the unbearable suffering of millions of people on the earth today. I know how I feel about it, and there have been times when the burden of it overwhelms me, but I have learned that I can also allow that same burden to energize me. If every Christian were to drown in the emotional flooding that occurs when we learn of mass suffering, we would all be on the couch staring at the wall and no one would be helped.

I am grateful for Christians around the world who contribute to improving the standard of living in cities, towns, and villages so that those who live there are safer, healthier, and better educated, giving hope to their children's future. And for many, they do not have the ability to travel and give in person. But many of us who give money should consider giving money and ourselves. Whatever we do on behalf of others, whenever possible, should create a relationship. When visiting refugee camps or orphanages in depressed areas, the biggest question on the minds of impoverished and suffering people is, "Will you return?" They may not always ask it, but they always think it. Returning to them builds credibility in you. It is a sign of the genuineness of your concern for them. When global engagement becomes a relationship between you and the person you help, the result is a transformation.

My generation, which makes up the majority of today's workforce, has arrived at one of those pivotal transition periods in human history. Let's take a brief look at what that means.

At no other time have individuals had the potential to interact with other people living in every continent on Earth or have the ability to engage in real time face-to-face conversations with several people who are situated in different parts of the world.

At no other time has one document been translated into every language, but within our lifetime we will witness the translation of the Bible into the more than six thousand spoken languages.

At no other time has world travel been as available, as rapid, or as safe as it is today. Nor have people been able to travel to far-off reaches of the world. There has never been another time in history when information (knowledge) has been so easily accessed by so many people of every nation and almost every class.

So, the question that we must ask ourselves is this: What are we going to do with these unique privileges? One option is that we use our unique possibilities to take advantage of people in other nations, mine their raw resources, and exploit their cheap labor. We could build empires by marketing cheap technological gadgets around the world. We could burn thousands of dollars— or tens of thousands, depending on our personal budgets—on cruises, exotic island resorts, safaris, or even attempting to climb

Mount Everest. We can jump into the billions-of-dollars-a-year Internet porn industry and make a killing (in more than one meaning of the term).

Or...

We could use this enhanced connectivity with humankind to introduce people to Jesus Christ and welcome them into the kingdom of God.

We could ensure that people who have access to the Bible in their own language are made aware of it. We could provide the necessary technology to get their hands on a Bible and ensure that they know how to read or how to use an app that reads it for them.

We could work on increasing and utilizing our vacation time to divide it between enjoyable leisure activities and providing humane services to others in the name of Jesus. By the way, children and especially teenagers typically find great pleasure in bringing food, water, and medicine to other children, especially once they have personally witnessed their impoverished conditions.

We can learn how to communicate the truth of God so that people are willing to listen. This may mean that we have to undo two hundred years of Christian evangelism by researching ways to get to the hearts and minds of today's non-Christian audiences and design creative strategies for doing this with the story of Jesus. Everyone who is right now reading these words already has the means to do this without spending a dime, taking time off from work, or crossing a street.

We can make certain that our food, clothing, perfumes and colognes, electronic gadgets, etc., do not come to our hands from the backs of oppressed men, women, and children.

Whatever decisions we make, we cannot wait for the answers to come from white, western males or historically evangelical organizations. The voices of Asia, Africa, South America, and Eastern Europe, and female voices, refugee voices, ethnic voices, and voices from the margins of society must be heard. That means that Christians who meet these criteria must raise their voices and join conversations.

The world that has been most affected by western nations—and this is especially true of the United States— needs a radical adjustment in values. It is often said that dictators and militant fundamentalists do not value human life. But corporate executives, entrepreneurs, and Wall Street financiers can be just as disinterested, lacking in empathy for others, and they have become some of the world's worst oppressors. These are also among the most miserable people in the world. Some of the happiest people are often among the poorest. The reason for this is that they keep close ties with the people they love, sharing meals, and engaging in meaningful family rituals. Many of us who were raised in mainstream America should live among people in other countries or families in the States who have maintained their strong ethnic ties in order to see how much we have missed. The needed adjustment of values is a revelation of how impoverished we are, in spite of our relative wealth, as families and communities.

"Go Therefore and Make Disciples of All the Nations"

Jesus' instructions regarding what the disciples were to do next sounded sedentary. As if now they needed to get up and get moving. My early Christian experience was influenced by a religious subculture that used Jesus' words—"Go therefore and make disciples of all nations" (Matthew 28:19)—to move me into the streets for cold-call evangelism or send me into the mission field with one of the usual Christian organizations. What Jesus said, however, was more like, "As you go," or, "On your journey, make disciples." We are already "on the go." The journey of our lives is taking us in many different directions. The road I travel each day may be near to your day-to-day environments, ten thousand miles away, or anywhere in between. But taking into consideration all of us who are in Christ Jesus, we pretty much cover the globe. So, when we begin looking for our mission field, do not be surprised if you find that you are already in it. Start making disciples!

If you live in a suburban neighborhood where everyone is either already Christian or over-evangelized pagans, consider the nearest inner city as a possible location to work "globally." This may be Seoul, South Korea; Oslo, Norway; New York City, New York; Johannesburg, South Africa; or Christchurch, New Zealand. Regardless of where in the world it may be, you can be certain that if it is a big city, it is also an international hub. Aside from the obvious needs in the slum and drug-infested areas of most every big city in the world, there are opportunities to show God's love to people of many different nations. Again, whether they live near or far, speak our language or not, share our diet or have their own exotic tastes, they are family. When I refer to our "family," I am referring to (a) those people who have already received the witness of God's Spirit and say that they are God's adopted children, and (b) those who do not yet know they could belong to the family of God.

nine
Practice #7: Make Disciples

In Robert Webber's book, *The Younger Evangelicals,* he observes that the church has been stuck too long with specific models that have been used to bring people to faith in Jesus Christ. The central idea is that nothing is more important for a person than knowing Jesus since, "There is salvation in no one else; for there is no other name under heaven that has been given among men by which we must be saved" (Acts 4:12). This means that if people are going to be rescued from hell, they must first believe in Jesus Christ as their "personal Lord and Savior," then *behave* like Jesus before they can *belong* to our Christian community. From these roots, systems have been designed to expose people to the basic details of sin, hell, Jesus' atoning death, forgiveness, and everlasting life. In earnest desire to quickly move them into our Christian community, we execute these strategies to help people make the most important decision of their lives as quickly as possible. Why? Because we desire them to belong to our Christian communities that otherwise they may not have been welcomed in if they hadn't chosen to believe in and behave like Jesus.

By seeing ourselves as Lifestyle Missionaries in our current culture, it would only seem fitting to sit, ask questions, and listen to those whom we are trying to share the message with in order to maximize our effectiveness. I have sat with countless friends who are not Christians, they have shared with me their perspective on many of these strategies. I will do my best to share my reflections and thoughts in an effort to inspire us to a deeper and larger paradigm on how we might understand and share the gospel of Jesus Christ today. In my years of ministry, I've noticed that there are two main methods that evangelicals use to spread Jesus' message: testifying and mass communication.

The first and most common method is called personal evangelism. Personal evangelism trains Christians to "testify" (share how this information has changed their lives) by witnessing to family and friends, in front of an audience, or out in the streets. Organizations like the Navigators and Campus Crusade and programs like Evangelism Explosion are known for helping believers become proficient in "spreading the gospel," "winning the lost," "reaching the world for Christ," and fulfilling "the Great Commission."

Another avenue is mass evangelism, in which the attempt is to communicate the Christian message to as many people as possible at one time and includes large rallies (sometimes referred to as "Crusades," which many today consider an unfortunate label), print publications (periodicals, comics, and books, especially Bibles), broadcasting through television and radio, and more recently social media.

In order to make these methods or any variation of these methods work, a simple and quick version of the gospel needed to be created. It has ranged from sharing the verse John 3:16 in speech or text, to a small booklet known as a "gospel tract." In these categories and much of what is found in between, I have many friends who work tirelessly and are seeing some success. But I have also found that many times in an effort to make the gospel "simple," we may have offered a smaller version of the gospel to our culture. This simpler version of the gospel has now lead to many Christian and post Christian cultures having a "been there, done that" mentality.

As a father of young children there is nothing worse then when one of my kids comes home from school sick. Immediately we go into panic mode and do our best to quarantine, while still loving, the infected child. Yet, nine out of ten times our efforts go to waste as we all end up catching the same virus. While we caught the virus in a moment, it takes over our entire schedules with multiple days of suffering. In many ways the gospel was meant to be a virus. A virus that would quickly infect all of humanity and take over our whole life. Unfortunately, in our desire to spread a simple gospel virus we've actually spread a weaker version of the intended life altering bigger gospel. This in turn has implicationally vaccinated our current cultural moment from that simple gospel message we share publicly. It's time for a deeper and broader understanding of the Gospel that's not just a verse but an entire story.

The story isn't just that man sinned, Jesus redeemed him and now we wait to enter heaven. That's only a two-part story. When looking at the whole of the bible we can see it as a four-part story. It's a story about a creator God who made creation (part 1) and said "it was good." Then the disorder of sin crept in (part 2) and separated man from his Creator. Yet, God sent His son to redeem (part 3) His creation. And now we are a part of joining the mission of Jesus to "make all things new" (part 4) by restoring order again as said in Revelation 21:5. Even today that gospel story is shaping my heart, mind and soul and will continue to until I'm with Jesus for eternity.

Now, in all seriousness, accepting the gospel into ones' heart is the biggest and most radically life-changing decision a person will ever make. Think for a moment about the situation we put people in when we press them for an answer to the question, "Will you accept Jesus as your Savior right now?" If someone expected me to make a huge decision that would affect the rest of my life, I would at least ask them if I could go home and sleep on it before giving my answer. So with sincere and properly motivated hearts, we approach strangers and offer them what can feel like an arranged marriage!

However, I am not saying that it is never appropriate to ask someone that we have known for only ten minutes if they want to become a Christian. There are times when the wheat fields are so ripe they practically harvest themselves. But we cannot make a convincing argument that the forms of evangelism I have described were the only models set down by Jesus and His apostles. At the very least, our Gospel needs to become bigger. The late Leon Morris, an Australian New Testament scholar said, "The gospel is as a pool in which a toddler can wade and yet an elephant can swim. It is both simple and profound. For the veriest beginner in the faith and for the mature Christian. Its appeal is immediate and never failing." The gospel is about a personal conversion experience, but it's also the ushering in of a kingdom meant to reorder the world back to the way God had intended it.

I agree with Webber that changing times call for new

models of mission. At the same time, I am not opposed to personal evangelism or mass evangelism, nor think that they are inherently wrong. In fact, I have joined hands with my friends in these endeavors. However, there tends to be a gaping hole in both the literature and practice of Christian evangelism. Dr. Charles Kraft indirectly pointed out the problem when he said, "At some point, the gospel must be incarnated." "Incarnated" means that a flesh and blood person who is filled with God's Spirit, living the gospel, and constantly sharing it with his or her life is also prepared to nurture the faith of anyone who chooses to respond to Jesus in them. A book, radio broadcast, television program, or giant public event cannot replace the necessary influence of a Christian living in one-to-one relationship with someone else whom God is drawing to Himself.

Perhaps you have heard the expression that someone "has a heart for the lost." What does that mean? It could be that a person feels deeply burdened over all the people in the world who do not know God or the grace, peace, and love that He pours into the believer. But feeling the weight of the multitudes who live without God is not the same thing as loving one individual in your own circles who does not know God and by your actions showing God's care to that person.

Impersonal Evangelism

Another concern that I have is when a new Christian is pressured into cutting off ties with his or her former family and friends unless they, too, become believers. While good intention is to help this new believer be renewed without distractions from his or her "past," at times this requirement can feel more cult-like than Christian. Jesus did not say to Matthew, "Follow me and give up all your old colleagues and friends." What we read is that Matthew invited Jesus into his home to introduce him to "many tax collectors and sinners" that came there to share a meal with Jesus and His disciples (Matthew 9:10).

Sanctification is not segregation. God's concern for the cleansing of my soul is that He separates me from my sins. If to live righteously with God we had to break off all contacts with non-Christians, "then you would have to go out of the world" (1 Corinthians 5:11).

Once someone is converted, they are often given a list of everyday religious duties, such as reading the Bible, attending Bible studies, praying, attending church, sharing their faith, and financially supporting their church and missionaries. At the same time, they must also adopt a lifestyle of instant and complete devotion to God, whereas those of us who have been Christians for many years are still working at dying to our ego, giving up lying, gossip and slander, and we are especially struggling to love our enemies. Young women must break up with non-Christian boyfriends. Young men must stop drinking or smoking. If you are new to the faith, the list of prohibitions goes on and on. In fact, you will have to master the elimination of all sin and appearance of evil before next Sunday in order to belong to the community of saints that one encounters in church. Make certain to dress appropriately, hide tattoos, and remove any signs of body piercing. Clean up in these ways and you will be able to hang out with us. Oh, and make sure you learn as quickly as possible why our church is the one true representation of Christianity in our community. It is best if you are able to explain this using our religious expressions and buzzwords.

That is the other side of impersonal (or depersonalized) evangelism. Not only have we heard the gospel delivered without much love, but new converts are quickly taught to behave in a way that can come across unloving. We begin by severing our relationships with anyone who is not a believer and next we inadvertently build walls between ourselves and believers who belong to other churches.

There are clusters of Christians (easily located on the Internet) who pride themselves on their doctrinal purity and their ability to soundly criticize and condemn well-known Christian leaders. The intense animosity they express, sometimes with expletives, is more indicative of antisocial personality disorder than Christian faith. It is hard not to think of the epic fail in evangelism that Jesus pointed out when He accused the scribes and Pharisees of traveling "around on sea and land to make one proselyte; and when he becomes one, you make him twice as much a son of hell as yourselves" (Matthew 23:15).

A good measure of the scandal of Jesus was not that He shut people out, but threw open the doors to let everyone in. He went so far as to promise that He would not deny anyone who came to Him. (John 6:37). When Jesus rolled into town, everyone belonged, even before they believed or behaved like a disciple. More than once the Pharisees and scribes grumbled, "This man receives sinners and eats with them" (Luke 15:2). In His parables, Jesus described the way that God's invitation was going out to everyone so that Jesus welcomed fishermen, children, lepers, Jewish tax collectors and Roman centurions, immoral women and violent men. Jesus was characterized as "a friend of sinners" (Luke 7:34).

How many of my friends are "sinners," that is to say, "non-Christians"? What did it mean that Jesus "received sinners and ate with them"? When it is believed that two lives bond by sharing a meal, then Jesus was associating with people outside the margin of the religious culture. But He had maintained His relationships with sinful humanity at the start in His baptism to the very end when "His grave was assigned with the wicked" (Isaiah 53:9). Jesus accepted sinners and spent time with them. They met. They shared food. Jesus was there for the sinner to talk, to struggle through issues together, and perhaps even joke around. These are all the things we do with our Christian friends, except Jesus did these things with the believers as well as the lost. And in order to win them to Himself, He revealed God to them, forgave their sins and invited them to enter God's kingdom.

On the flip side, Jesus warned the leading religious people that they were in for a surprise. When they would find themselves locked out of the kingdom, which they presumed was theirs, while they would watch people from the four corners of the world coming and entering the kingdom (Luke 13:28–29).

Walking People into Faith

How can we disciple people into faith? I think we could research the Scriptures and come up with a lot of good ideas, but any method, formula, or curriculum would depend on one central requirement: we must be *living the Christian faith* ourselves.

Jesus knew that He could enter any environment where humans were present and not be compromised by it or fall into the temptations presented there. Jesus knew whom He was and never took a break from being true to Himself. If He was in a room full of tax collectors and prostitutes, He knew why He was there and what He would do. Rather than find Himself shadowed in their darkness, He bathed them in His light.

If we know our true selves in Jesus, it is possible for us to welcome many people into our circle of friends regardless of what they believe or how they behave. As long as we are true to ourselves and to our Lord, the friends in our group would have opportunity to observe our faith, hear our prayers, see us turn to the Scriptures, continue in our transformation, work for a change in our world, carry an inner peace, and bless those around us. Then, it is possible our friends, like those sinners who made their way to Jesus, might say to themselves, "This looks real. I have seen the story and heard the song. I want in!"

Here is an example: Campbell Hill was a pastor in New Zealand who grew tired of not having a significant connection with people outside of his church walls. He resigned and took a job at a nearby convenience store. He also walked his dog around the neighborhood, praying for opportunities to share his faith. Two weeks into Campbell's neighborhood walks, his wife called his cell phone. Panic laced her voice. "Cam, where are you? Come home now. We've been robbed!"

Campbell sprinted home where he found the front door broken. The police were taking statements and his wife was severely shaken. The officer in charge informed Campbell that the robber would most likely return, so he should watch for him. In event that the robber did return, Campbell was encouraged to immediately call the authorities so they could catch the thief.

A week passed but the robber hadn't returned. In the meantime, Campbell went back to the streets and his prayers. He desperately wanted to introduce one of his neighbors to God. A couple weeks went by when he received another urgent call from his wife. "Campbell, it is happening again!" Quickly he called the police as he ran home.

This time, the thief was apprehended. It turned out to be a teenage Maori. The police gave Campbell a court date and told him he needed to show up for it to press charges against the teenager. On the day of the hearing, the judge asked, "Mr. Hill, would you like to press charges against the offender?"

Campbell's response surprised everyone in the courtroom, even himself. As he stood to respond to the judge, he was struck by an idea that wrapped up everything he had been wanting and praying for in the previous two or three months. "Yes, your honor," he said, "I would like to press charges. If it pleases the court, I request that he does his community service at my home and under my supervision." With a strike of the gavel, the judge granted his request and passed the sentence.

The next day, Campbell's doorbell rang, and standing there was the young man ready to serve his first day of community service. He was wearing one of the shirts he had taken from Campbell's closet! Shaking his head, Campbell stepped outside and pointed to the fence they were going to paint together. Over the following weeks, the teenager got to know Campbell and his family, which led to the opportunity to meet the young man's family.

That young man was the first answer Campbell received to his prayer. He was the first person from the community outside the church that he introduced to Jesus Christ. The young man's family also came into the faith.

Campbell realized how God was rewriting his life's story. He discovered that his willingness to join Jesus in His mission to those who lived near the Campbell home resulted in unexpected opportunities to share his faith. With two friends, Campbell co-founded Good Neighbor, an organization that is "Helping neighbors transform their communities" (https://www.goodneighbour.co.nz/). Campbell Hill began serving God locally in a way that is seeding global ministry.

Everyone has the opportunity to belong to the family

of God through Jesus Christ. Some people understand this and others have yet to understand it. Regardless, Jesus' death was a signed adoption certificate provided for all humankind, so that by His Spirit they could have the opportunity to come into the shelter of God the Father. Are we going to continue to deny the adoption of others by closing the door to them with our "Christian Only" clubs and events? How will they know of this opportunity if we are not the ones opening our doors to share it with them?

One of my favorite examples of Jesus' inclusiveness is Simon Peter ("Simon" is his given name at birth, and "Peter" is the name Jesus gave him). In renaming Peter, Jesus redefined him, revealing the person he would become in Christ, his true self. But the encouraging feature of Peter's story is that he stubbornly remained both sides of himself for a long time. He could be the rock who discerned the truth of Jesus by a direct revelation from God, and then he would immediately become the mouthpiece of Satan. One moment his mind was set on God's interests and in the next it was set on human interests (Matthew 16:16-17; 22-23). He was both his old self and his new self at the same time.

Under normal circumstances, discipleship refers to a period of education and training at the feet of a recognized rabbi (cf. Acts 22:3). However, when it comes to being a disciple of Jesus, discipleship does not run for one season of our lives but is ongoing. In fact, the late philosopher and Christian writer, Dallas Willard, believed that our spiritual development continues through all eternity. It is at least certain that we cannot reach perfection in this life. This means that we need to be patient with ourselves and with others as well.

Simon Peter was a fisherman, not a scribe or student of the law. Even after Jesus' resurrection, it was obvious to Jerusalem's elite that Peter and John "were uneducated and untrained men." What explained their confidence and made them stand out was not their intellectual achievements, but the fact that they had "been with Jesus" (Acts 4:13). Do we regret not having a degree in theology or at least a better knowledge of the Bible? Perhaps. Do we feel remorse for our spiritual failures and sins? Of course, at least that is the normal response of the believer. But those are not the actions or issues that define us. Those are merely the growing pains of the transformation from our old self to our new self. Our discipleship is ongoing. Whether or not we have a higher education is of no concern to Jesus. His joy is to take us as we are and make us into what He wants us to be. He wants us to be students without ever becoming "graduates" of His school. He is neither surprised nor crushed when Peter acts like Simon. He simply points it out and moves on, while His other disciples continue to follow behind.

We cannot allow ourselves to get stuck in excessive guilt, shame, or self-condemnation. Everyone is flawed, and we all experience the same types of emotions and feelings. It is up to us as believers to have faith that Jesus will care for us in our darkest times.

Anxiety does not accomplish or produce anything that is useful.

As emotions, guilt and shame cannot effectively promote spiritual growth.

Condemnation, whether heaped on you by others or by yourself, does not motivate greater effort or inspire higher goals.

Jesus tells you again and again, "Do not be afraid," "Do not be anxious," "I do not condemn you," "Your sins are forgiven," "I am with you."

According to the Gospels, the Lord's first and last words

to Peter were, "Follow Me" (Matthew 4:19; John 21:22). Jesus does not command us to lead the charge, to take over His position as Messiah, to be more than we are capable of being. He asks us to follow Him, which, given our human nature, turns out to be difficult enough. When we sin, get lost or confused, wake up in a bad mood, have no idea what we are to do next, the solution is clear: Get back to Jesus and follow Him.

There is nothing you can confess to Jesus that He does not already know. Jesus was the first to inform Peter that he would deny his Lord three times before the rooster announced the next sunrise. I do not doubt that Peter's denial was painful for Jesus in his hour of rejection, but it was no surprise (Luke 22:60-61). Jesus did not give up on Peter in spite of his refusal to own his relationship to his Lord. It would seem, however, that Peter had given up on himself when he told several other disciples, "I am going fishing" (John 21:3). It was like saying, "Well, I tried to follow Jesus, but I failed. I am too much of a coward. I never was that much of a religious person and it was silly of me to think I could actually be part of something as big and wonderful as the kingdom of heaven. I'm going back to what I know: the sea, the ship, and my fishing nets." He left Peter behind and returned to being Simon.

When Jesus finally took him aside, the first thing He did was use his old name, "Simon, son of John, do you love Me more than these?" Ouch! That is the man Peter had been when Jesus found him. He bore the name and the relationship to his father that had defined him. But Jesus was not engraving the name Simon in stone. He was offering him the opportunity to be something more, to be the man he was in Jesus' eyes and heart. It was an invitation to finally move beyond that. As difficult as it was for Peter to overcome his humiliation and feeling that he had no right to ever again ask Jesus to trust him, he managed to step up and say, "Lord, You know all things; You know that I love You." And with that, Jesus put him back to work.

As we read through this conversation, tinged with intense passion, we notice something interesting. From the beginning of the story, John refers to Peter as "Simon Peter" and does so again when Jesus encounters and addresses him on the shore (John 21:2–3, 11, 15). Then, after Jesus and Peter ended their dialogue, John drops the "Simon" and it is "Peter" who turns to see another disciple and "Peter" who asks Jesus about that other man. We can be sure that Peter felt miserable through that dialogue with Jesus, but we plainly see that the rupture in his relationship with Jesus had been repaired. He was restored to his true self and the meaning of his life that he found in following Jesus. Most significant of all is that Jesus did this for Peter's sake and not His own. The Lord had never let go of Peter. And He has never let go of you.

Get that into your heart and head, and you will be able to bounce back from any time of trial, trouble, or failure.

Peter belonged to Jesus and he belonged among the apostles. We know the powerhouse he became later in the Spirit and the thousands of people in Jerusalem who received Jesus after Peter's first sermon. We know how he stood up to the very people who crucified Jesus, which sent Peter into denial and tearful remorse as he proclaimed to them the name of Jesus. But look at the time and trials that it took for Peter to get to this point! If he had waited until these accomplishments would be counted among the apostles, he would have never made it. It was after his years with Jesus, his vacillating between Simon and Peter, false self and true self—which did not end here (cf. Galatians 2:11-14)—and much mentoring by Jesus that he grew into a strong

Christian. So how can we possibly expect to see a person become a Christian and earn a place among the followers of Jesus in the space of a day? We cannot go and lead people to Christ outside of our church walls and then leave them there.

Now we are about to explode into our world, the new people of God, filled with His love and empowered by His Spirit. But before we leave this moment, I want to reiterate these points:

Making disciples means not giving up on people. Being a disciple is not giving up on ourselves and depends more on God's work in us than our "works of righteousness." The affection Jesus Christ has toward us never fails. We may choose to run from Him for a while or ignore His voice, but it is never the other way around. He will never leave us or forsake us. That is true for those of us who consider ourselves Christians and those not yet.

Grasping the truth of all this is life eternal and abundant. Living the truth of it is transformation. We are changed. Others are changed. One day, the whole world will be changed. Jump in now. Be on the cutting edge of the dawn of this new day.

ten
"As You Are Already Going…"

My hope is that I've inspired you to see how incredibly valuable your life is to the mission of Jesus. He is on a mission all around you, beckoning you to come and join Him on that mission. Why? So you can be His incarnated hands, feet, and voice to those around you who are being touched by Jesus. Remember, it's His mission, not your mission. Take comfort in the fact that it's not about what you "have to" do but what you "get to" do. Here are just a few simple, practical, and immediate ways to apply these seven practices to your life. After all, I'm not calling you to get up and go because you are already going.

As you are already going ask God to show you the mission He is on where you live and spend most of your time. Begin to look around at the people who are there. You will definitely see someone who does not yet know Jesus Christ. Pray that God will lead you to those who are most open and prepared to receive what God has for them.

As you are already going focus on one person and pray for him or her. What you want first is to get to know them without labeling them. See if you can befriend that person. Be natural and treat them as you would any of your friends. Let them be whoever they are, not as what you think they should be or hope they will become. You do not have to condone anyone's sin, but neither do you have to judge them. Know that their beliefs are different from yours. Be curious about what they believe. Do not worry or get angry if they reject your beliefs. Choose your battles carefully.

As you are already going be YOU! Be your true self, the person you are in Jesus Christ, His new creation. Live the kingdom, whatever the cost. Invite others to come along for the ride. Give them a place at the table with you and your Christian friends. Do not assume they will not join you. Be a normal person; there is no need to act like a saint. Most breakdowns between Christians and non-Christians occur in Christian brains and not in the real world.

As you are already going, point it out when God is obviously doing something in a person's life whether or not he or she is a Christian. Do not break a battered reed or put out a smoldering wick (Matthew 12:20), but as much as it is in your power to do so, fan the spark into a flame. Such things are no coincidence in the presence of God. Let them know that God is sending us these moments of grace. This is the thing when you have a relationship with them.

As you are already going commit yourself to them in friendship. This is the point of being a follower of Jesus—reconciliation, turning enemies into friends, finding long-lost brothers and sisters and leading them home. It may be that in helping them understand that Jesus gave His life for them, you may need to give your life for them also. Attend their weddings, share car pools, raise your children together. Consider a sports club, a ship cruise with older people (if it is within your means), play with a company softball team. Just do everything to the glory of God in the name of Jesus but without overstating your message.

As you are already going remind yourself that your mission is a lifestyle, not a weekend pastime; that walking with Jesus is a journey, not a destination. Eternity breaks into here and now and is not waiting for us somewhere in the future. The Spirit of God is a person we can experience now, not merely a doctrine we believe in. Do not forget, we are in this for life!

In closing, if you feel inspired by this book, please feel free to email me to dialogue more or to connect in a deeper way to our tribe. Here is my personal email: actifist@gmail.com!

I wish you all success. God bless!
Matt Whitlock

Made in the USA
San Bernardino, CA
15 January 2019